Text Copyright © Darren McKellin
All rights reserved. No part of this g
form without permission in writing 1
case of brief quotations embodied in (

Legal & Disclaimer
The information contained in this book and its contents is not designed to replace or take the place of any form of medical or professional advice; and is not meant to replace the need for independent medical, financial, legal, or other professional advice or services, as may be required. The content and information in this book have been provided for educational and entertainment purposes only.

The content and information contained in this book have been compiled from sources deemed reliable, and it is accurate to the best of the Author's knowledge, information, and beliefs. However, the author cannot guarantee its accuracy and validity, and cannot be held liable for any errors and/or omissions. Further, changes are periodically made to this book as and when needed. Where appropriate and/or necessary, you must consult a professional (including but not limited to your doctor, attorney, financial advisor, or such other professional advisor) before using any of the suggested remedies, techniques, or information in this book.

Upon using the contents and information contained in this book, you agree to hold harmless the Author from and against any damages, costs, and expenses, including any legal fees potentially resulting from the application of any of the information provided by this book. This disclaimer applies to any loss, damages, or injury caused by the use and application, whether directly or indirectly, of any advice or information presented, whether for breach of contract, tort, negligence, personal injury, criminal intent, or under any other cause of action.

You agree to accept all risks of using the information presented inside this book.

You agree that by continuing to read this book, where appropriate and/or necessary, you shall consult a professional (including but not limited to your doctor, attorney, or financial advisor or such other advisor as needed) before using any of the suggested remedies, techniques, or information in this book.

TABLE OF CONTENTS

CHAPTER 1
MINDFULNESS MOVEMENT 8

CHAPTER 2
EARTH BOOK 14
  1. The Art of Wealth 18
  2. Work Harder on Yourself 19
  3. Silence and Meditation 23
  4. Direction 28
  5. Dream Big 31
  6. Intention 31
  7. Revenge and Karma 36
  8. Remove Limitations 38
  9. Full Moon, New Moon Intention 42

CHAPTER 3
FIRE BOOK 44
  1. The Art of War 48
  2. De-escalation 49
  3. The Art of Healthy Conflict 51
  4. Motivation 53
  5. Maslow's Hierarchy of Needs 54
  6. Teamwork 56
  7. Characteristics of Successful Sales Managers 57
  8. Selling 61
  9. Accountability in Sales 63
  10. Competition 63
  11. Sales Process 65

CHAPTER 4
WATER BOOK **66**
   1. The Art of Communication 71
       a. Inner Dialogue.................................. 71
       b. Communicating with Others.......................... 72
   2. Gossip and Confidentiality............................ 74
   3. The Art of Avoiding Arguments......................... 74
   4. Balance 76
   5. Focus and Listening 79
   6. Do Less 80
   7. Change 80

CHAPTER 5
WIND BOOK **82**
   1. Reading People 86
   2. Achieving Power.................................. 89
   3. Hiring, Discipline and Firing 90
   4. Obstacles 93
   5. Effortless Success 93
   6. Associates....................................... 96
   7. Meetings.. 97

CHAPTER 6
AIR BOOK **100**
   1. Mind, Body and Spirit 104
   2. Executive Presence................................ 109
   3. Vibrations and Aura............................... 110
   4. Humility 112
   5. Leading and Coaching 113
   6. Power of Baked Bread and Birthdays.................... 114

CHAPTER 7
CONCLUSION **116**

> "YOU CAN'T STOP THE WAVES, BUT YOU CAN LEARN TO SURF."

JON KABAT-ZINN

DEDICATED TO
My parents Jim and Carolyn,
who are in their eighties, and do yoga every day.

SPECIAL THANKS TO
Jon James Lynch, Doug Hymas, Mike Alfant, Paul Dupuis,
Jim Weisser, Andrew Silberman, Lowell Sheppard, Mike Carroll,
Saleh B, Robert Heldt, Simon Farrell and Leroy Norby.

CHAPTER 1

MINDFULNESS MOVEMENT

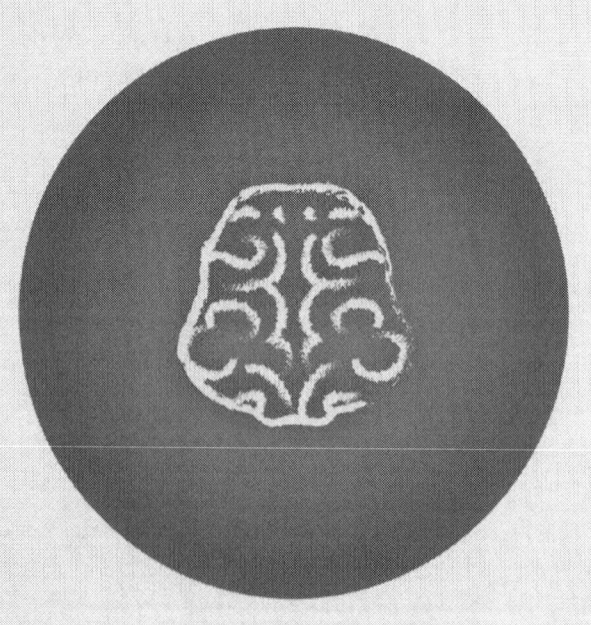

MINDFULNESS MOVEMENT

Thousands of sales books exist, covering prospecting, pipeline building, and closing. However, there are very few books that cover the mindful and spiritual aspects of achieving sales and career success. Through the application of **mindfulness**, leaders have been shown to foster teamwork, deliver results, and form a deeper connection with their careers and their lives. This book is filled with the principles of mindfulness to empower you to lead a more fulfilling and successful life and career.

Thirty years ago, I moved to Japan and started a career in IT sales before moving to leadership. I have built and run high-performing sales teams for organizations, such as Verizon, Oracle, NetSuite, and Zscaler. To do this in Japan meant that I had to learn to function in one of the world's most challenging, unique, and opaque cultures. As a transplanted Westerner, I had to learn an entirely new way of business from the ground up, much of it from trial and error. Living and working in the East taught me the importance of team harmony, being patient, and waiting for the right timing. I discovered my work life and career success reflected in my personal life, and noticed those who are highly organized with their business ventures mirror this tendency in other aspects of their existence.

Twenty years ago, if I had walked into a job interview and mentioned that I meditate, I would have been met with skeptical looks and probably lost the job opportunity. When interviewing at Oracle Japan in 2016, I decided I would talk about mindfulness techniques and meditation. To my surprise, I was met with a positive response and ended up with a better role than the one I originally was contacted about. The final interview was with the hiring manager, as well as the VP who would later become my boss. The interview went smoothly, and I was hired for the job I wanted. Later, when I began to learn more about Oracle's interview process, I noticed that I had not been asked any questions related to ethics. I asked my boss about this, and he responded: "Early on in your interview, you mentioned that you do a lot of meditation. At this point, I felt a sense of vulnerability and honesty about you and decided that I could trust you fully. This led me to skip the ethics questions." I was amazed! The mention of meditation had strengthened my chances of being hired.

A key concept I learned in the East is that less is more, which is not common in the West. For example, on a sales call, talk less—then the customer can speak more. When faced with a crisis or a problem, almost every Western manager I ever had asked: "What action are you taking to resolve it?" They didn't consider the fact that taking no action is also an option and maybe the best way forward. If left alone, problems often find a way of getting resolved on their own. Instead of asking "what action," ask your staff "is this an action-inducing issue?" If action is not required, then do nothing and monitor the situation. If action is required, then clearly define and communicate the next steps.

Our work life and career success reflect in our personal life. If you decide to learn how to listen keenly to your customers at work, you may also find yourself listening carefully to your partner or kids at home. Likewise, starting a daily exercise program will provide more stamina, which will help you be more productive and alert at work. Mindfulness helps us to control our conditioned responses by allowing us to take a pause, be present, and choose the best way to act in any situation. In business, being controlled and measured in your responses is a distinguishing quality that employers look for.

The five chapters in this book pay homage to Miyamoto Musashi, who wrote his classic samurai strategy book, *The Book of Five Rings*, more than 500 years ago. Musashi was born a samurai in the 16th century and is known as one of Japan's greatest swordsmen, winning more than 60 life-and-death battles. He was also a distinguished painter, philosopher, and strategist. At the end of his life, he wrote his masterpiece, which is still popular and relevant today. It is considered a classic treatise on military strategy, much like Sun Tzu's *The Art of War*, and has influenced businesspeople and strategists over the years. The book teaches the universal essence of the pursuit of any path toward mastery.

Musashi's classic focuses on mastering one's craft—in his case, the martial arts—and has found an audience in the business world. He divided his book based on the five elements: Earth, Fire, Water, Wind, and Air. Using these elements, he describes his style of sword fighting. As in Musashi's classic, each chapter in this book is also based on the five distinct elements. Each element has its own characteristic and meaning that relates to strategy and business.

THE EARTH BOOK — Base, Foundation, Planning, Direction; Being grounded to the Earth.

THE WATER BOOK — Flexibility, Change, Fluidity, Communication; Adapting to any space as water does.

THE FIRE BOOK — Conflict, Passion, Motivation, Drive; Desire for success that courses through the body like wildfire.

THE WIND BOOK — Style, Strategy; Winds of change blowing in a new era.

THE AIR BOOK — Emptiness, Presence, Potentiality; Enlightenment requires complete inner silence.

For example, imagine that you are entering a meeting and you do not want to be swayed from your position, so you choose to focus on the Earth element. Five minutes before the meeting, imagine yourself as an immovable rock: really feel it. This will help you be grounded and steady as the meeting progresses, and will help solidify your position in front of the other attendees. In a different scenario, before a meeting with a sales team, you may take a few minutes to focus on the Fire element and feel the passion burning in you. By doing this, the sales team will be able to feel your desire, which will, in turn, inspire them to efforts that go beyond 100 percent.

CHAPTER

EARTH BOOK

> "MOVE AS SWIFTLY AS THE WIND AND CLOSELY FORMED AS THE WOOD. ATTACK LIKE THE FIRE AND BE STILL AS THE MOUNTAIN."
>
> **SUN TZU,** *THE ART OF WAR*

EARTH BOOK

Musashi describes the essence of the Earth (ground) book as the foundation for mastery. "Know the smallest things and the biggest things, the shallowest things, and the deepest things. As if it were a straight road mapped out on the ground, the first book is called the Ground book." In English, we similarly advise people to "stay grounded," or "keep your feet on the ground." One must have a firm foundation upon which they can build their mastery. In the Earth Book, we establish the base of where we are going, and why are we pursuing a particular path. We must also set a precise mindset, which we can later expand upon to achieve success.

The element of Earth is crucial in the world of sales and business. Sales careers are turbulent and disorienting, with massive changes taking place seemingly overnight. Without the proper planning, direction, and intentions, it is easy for you to get swept off your feet. This section of the book teaches the following:

1. Grounding yourself by organizing your goals, intentions, and dreams
2. Grounding yourself through meditation and self-improvement
3. Grounding yourself by overcoming fear and stress

THE ART OF WEALTH

There is no reason that one cannot be extremely wealthy and, at the same time, be a balanced, thoughtful person who makes a positive impact on society. Before we can even begin to talk about your goals and pursuits, we first need to ensure that you are in the correct state of mind to improve your career and your life. The Earth element calls for the proper mindset; but if you continue to think that you are not deserving of wealth and fortune, it will be difficult to improve yourself mindfully.

You must understand that if you have good intentions, it is, in fact, virtuous to aim for wealth. If your loved ones are being harmed or there are injustices taking place around you, having no resources makes it very difficult to help. Society and individuals will sometimes try to make us feel guilty or "greedy" for wanting to get ahead. Never, ever, feel guilty for striving to be successful in your career and life.

When we create wealth, we employ others and purchase goods, which in turn keeps finance circulating and helps the economy expand. Individuals who create wealth are, in fact, aiding society. We live in an amazingly progressive era, where starting a new business is easier than ever before. Cloud technologies are lowering barriers to entry in many industries. Take publishing for example: now just about anyone can promote their ideas online by self-publishing books and printing on demand. Opportunities are abundant for those who are proactive and have the drive to succeed. Our universe has always provided us with what we need to succeed, so it is within your reach to grow, prosper, and make a positive impact on those around you. Many people are familiar with a commonly misquoted verse from the Bible, "Money is the root of all evil." But in fact, the real quote states: "**The love of money** is the root of all evil."

Now, unashamedly and without guilt or reservation, go forth and prosper.

WORK HARDER ON YOURSELF

Instinctively, most workers think they need to work harder at their job to get ahead. Instead of managing four projects, they work on five. Instead of working eight hours a day, they work 10. This plan backfires if you become too valuable in your current role to be moved. If you work hard on your job, you can make a living. If you work hard on yourself and increase your skills, you can make a fortune. There are two areas of focus for improving skill sets. The first and most important factor is to solidify your strong points, and the second is to identify any weaknesses in your current skill set that are holding you back from getting your ideal job.

Improvements could be as simple as watching a series of videos on YouTube on a relevant work topic. Or it could be something quantifiable, such as getting a degree that could boost your worth in your chosen field. One of the main areas that can help people in any profession is getting comfortable with public speaking. According to American investor and business tycoon Warren Buffet: "You can improve your value by 50 percent just by learning communication skills—public speaking." Public speaking is a universal skill that can help workers in almost every profession.

1. Fixing the Weakest Links

Your career can only rise to the level of the weakest link in your skill set. Make a list of the six or seven skills that are mandatory to succeed at your dream job, then identify the skill that you are least competent in. You will need to work on this skill until you have brought it up to a certain minimum level to successfully perform in the role.

In my school years, I always struggled with math. Several years ago when I first heard of the concept of raising the weakest link in one's skill set, I realized that to become a senior executive in any company, especially in sales, I would need to be proficient in tracking, analyzing, forecasting, and reporting figures. I spent numerous hours studying spreadsheets and I volunteered to take the lead on many of the routine forecasting activities on the team. Within a couple of years, I improved to the point where mathematics and figures were no longer a weakness.

A few years later, I identified a need to improve my Japanese language skills to be considered for senior roles in the Japanese job market. I went to Japanese school part-time, studied on my own, and volunteered to make speeches in Japanese to various organizations. In both cases, I put in a strong effort to raise my weaknesses. Not surprisingly, new doors opened for me and I received the promotions and career path I wanted.

2. Focus on Your Strengths

While trying to improve your skill set, many people tend to focus only on eliminating their weaknesses. Schools teach students to shore up their weaknesses from an early age; we are conditioned to obsess over our flaws. If a student struggles with math or English, they may enroll themselves in remedial classes or get tutoring. In other words, they will spend an inordinate amount of time on subjects they are not naturally good at. But what if schools took a different approach? Let's assume this child who is struggling in math or English is a musical prodigy or has an affinity for digital technology. It would be better if schools helped students improve upon their natural talents and encouraged them to pursue what they are passionate about.

Focus on what you're good at instead of wasting too much time doing things you're bad at. This may sound contradictory to what I said earlier about improving your weaknesses, but it is crucial to distinguish between the improvements that are within your reach and the ones that are not. Many people think their talents are innate gifts, so they never strive to improve them. However, with some persistence, strengths can be turned into super-strengths. Talent should be nurtured, and improving strengths is a lot more rewarding in the long run than working on weaknesses that bring a lower payoff.

Identifying strengths can be tricky. In my case, from an early age, I knew I was a "people person." In the workplace, I knew I had a high emotional quotient (EQ), which meant I got along well with others. I knew this was a strength and, as such, never tried to improve my people skills. Slowly, I began to learn that if I studied more about what makes people tick and what motivates them, I could become even more effective at my job.

One good way to identify strengths is to ask your boss, colleagues, friends, and family for honest feedback. Praise for work that comes easily to you is another sign. Perhaps you are good at compiling data and making presentations for meetings. Take an hour or two out of your day, go online, and study how the best presentations are made. In just one or two hours, you could learn numerous tricks and ideas that could boost your presentation skills and impress the higher-ups.

Just remember to never stop learning and never stop improving. If your current employer doesn't appreciate your improvements, then there's another employer out there who might. Identify the key weakness or weaknesses holding you back, improve them to the minimum level required for success, and then go all-in on your strengths to help you move ahead.

ACTIVITY

Compile a list of your strengths and weaknesses in your particular field.

In front of each bullet point in your list, write down activities that can help you improve them.

It could be as simple as watching a YouTube video, taking an online course or a part-time class, or doing practice questions for 30 minutes each day.

Being aware of all the resources you have to help improve yourself is the first step to bettering your skill set.

SILENCE & MEDITATION

If you wish to truly ground yourself and achieve inner stability and peace, you need to spend time in silence. For thousands of years humanity survived without iPhones. Our time was spent sitting in a field watching our crops go, or patiently waiting for our prey to wander into the range of our crude bows. Modern society went through a massive change, and now we are wired 24/7. The first and last thing we think to do in our day is to check our phones. For some people, almost every waking minute is spent with some sort of external stimulus.

We have long lived without technological distractions and most of our day was spent connected with our inner dialogue—a form of speech that is the best connection we have to ourselves. Now, we are tuned in with our devices and tuned out from our inner selves. I'm here to show you how reverting to that state of complete silence or meditation for a minimum of 10–20 minutes a day can bring a huge change in your life.

Time and time again, I read about geniuses and creative folks such as Thomas Edison and Albert Einstein, who claimed that they got their best ideas in the shower. Why is that? Is water a magical facilitator of brilliant thoughts? Maybe so, but I believe the shower is one of the few times in our day when we escape the constant external influx of stimulation, and our inner dialogue naturally surfaces. Along with it comes the ideas our subconscious mind wishes to bring to the conscious mind.

In the shower, Edison had little external distractions and his internal dialogue could unleash his most creative thoughts. Had Edison practiced meditation for 20 minutes a day, it could have had a similar or perhaps even greater impact. Sitting in silence for 20 minutes will allow us to connect to the magic of what our subconscious mind wants us to know. Some of what we see in our dreams, remembered or forgotten, can arise during quiet time.

I have interviewed scores of successful people to get content for this book. Almost all of them had a routine of quiet time or meditation, usually in the morning before the day gets busy. Most arise early and have a set routine they go through. I go through a morning routine before opening any emails or starting any work-related activities. I make a pot of hot tea and a glass of warm lemon water and sit in silence for 30–60 minutes each morning. Sometimes I'm sitting on a meditation pillow and am very serious about avoiding distractions. At other times, I'm sitting in a chair drinking tea and lemon water. No iPhone, no external stimulus, no distractions. It is the best part of my day almost every day. I take this opportunity to brainstorm solutions for a problem, or I sit in quiet and perform focused meditation to clear my head entirely.

You might think to yourself: "But I can't meditate! I tried and it didn't work." No one is born an expert at meditating. Every person has to start from scratch, which means we all start with a racing or uncontrollable mind at the beginning. Remember that the benefits of meditation are endless, yet it is so easy that it only requires two skills. You need only to be able to breathe and sit. For some, it might be sitting cross-legged on the floor, for others, it might be 20 minutes with a cup of tea. It could even be a 30-minute walk in the morning. Until your mind slows down, you will not have the clarity or patience to advance. The slower you go, the quicker you advance. Rushing around without quiet time to make sure you are going in the correct direction will only hold you back.

As a famous meditation-related saying goes: "Everyone should meditate for 30 minutes a day, and if they are too busy, then they should meditate for 60 minutes a day."

Meditation helps to unleash your creative side. Many times, in silence, answers to an issue tend to appear. Find time to be quiet and listen within. Try to do it every day; mornings are usually best as you manage to meditate before you can get swept away into the world of news alerts and emails. The ultimate aim of awareness is to be in the present: here and now. Nothing exists in the past. Nothing exists in the future—it hasn't happened. The only reality that exists is in the present. There is only now.

Overstimulated minds resemble the water of a pond which has been disturbed by a stick. It can be cloudy, and you can hardly see the bottom of the pond due to the ripples that appear. Once the pond becomes calm, however, the silt and mud descend to the bottom, and the water becomes transparent. If someone drops a rock into the pond, the mud gets stirred up again, and it takes time for the water to become clear. Similarly, in silence, our minds become clear, and we can see the path that we should be taking.

More than two decades ago when I first began meditating, I noticed I had become more relaxed in my life. This concerned me for a multitude of reasons; I relied on my aggressive leadership style to achieve sales, and my assertive personality was what gave me a competitive edge in the business world. Since then, I've come to believe that the key lies in shifting effortlessly between a relaxed state of mind and a highly motivated spirit in an instant, and I hope that by the end of this book you will be able to achieve both states with ease.

ACTIVITY

Wake up a little earlier tomorrow and do not turn on the TV or check email.

Avoid speaking or getting into long conversations.

Get some water and/or a hot drink and find a place where you can sit in silence.

Keep your mind and spirit quiet and calm. When the external stimulus is removed, answers will start to appear to you.

Then do this the next day, and the day after that, and make it part of your daily routine and your success will grow.

> "THE WORLD MAKES WAY FOR THE MAN WHO KNOWS WHERE HE IS GOING."
>
> **RALPH WALDO EMERSON**

DIRECTION

Before we can drive our career to excellence and our life to balance and satisfaction, we need to make sure we're heading in the right direction. The most important part of grounding yourself is knowing the path you are on, and where it will take you. This way, there will be no unexpected gust of wind that can sweep you off your feet. To start with, can you name your career and life goals? If you can't, you need to start today. Without this in mind, you will surely end up somewhere unsatisfactory. When you begin identifying your career and life goals, you might not come up with all the answers immediately, but you need to start somewhere. Ask yourself these questions:

- What do I want in life?
- What is my life's purpose?
- How can I be of benefit to society? My family? My company?

Material wealth and money are totally fine to have as goals. However, money alone almost always leaves one unsatisfied. Goals-based upon money, material items, or sex are outside of you and will only make you happy temporarily. Your list should include items such as personal growth and improved relationships.

ACTIVITY

Find somewhere to think. Head out to a coffee shop, a bench in a park or a quiet place in your house.

- Write down the top 10 things you want in life.

- Write down your life's purpose in one sentence, if possible. The shorter the text, the harder it is.

- Write down as many ways you can be a benefit to society, your family and your company.

"YOU CAN ONLY GROW TO THE SIZE OF YOUR THOUGHTS."

BENJAMIN FRANKLIN

DREAM BIG

Think small, and small will be delivered. Think grand, and that is what you will get. Make your goals big. If you could have anything you wanted, what would it be? Start there. What do you really want?

Great accomplishments are not achieved by accident. Steve Jobs did not create the iPhone by accident. Dream big because then you know you are going to be big. Do you have your dream in mind? Good. Take that dream, and now inflate it. What if it were to become 10—no, 100 times bigger! If your current dream is to earn two million, then dream of earning $20 million. Then brainstorm in your quiet time: "What are the ways I could make $20 million?" This helps make it real. Consider it plausible with your thoughts, feelings and actions. Visualize the result in your head as if it has already been achieved. Live as if your desire has already been achieved. If you want wealth, imagine that you are already wealthy. Dream big—and then dream bigger.

INTENTION

Henry Ford said, "Whether you think you can or think you can't, you're right." Once you have an idea of your goals and purpose, visualization is the key to bringing it to life. Intention and visualization are the starting points to achieving your goals. Everything mankind has created was first visualized in someone's mind. Having an intention, visualizing it, and making yourself and the Earth aware of it can help you remain on your feet, so you can keep progressing on the path to success.

Intentions and goals need to be specific as the universe does not respond well to vague messages. Instead of saying "I want to be rich" or "I want to hit my sales target" phrase it more specifically. Say with conviction: "I will achieve 150 percent of my target in Q1 and 200 percent in Q2" or, "By the age of 45, I will be VP of my company and will have a net worth of more than $2 million."

Visualizing your intentions and goals is powerful. However, "feeling" them takes it to the next level. For example, if your goal is to have

$5 million, how would you feel if you already had that money in your bank account? I'm guessing that any stress you have about finances would fall away. You need to feel the goal, already present at your fingertips, to enter the state of mind that would help you achieve it.

Visualize it: have your body imagine what it would be like to walk into a store and buy the one item you have always wanted but could never afford. Imagine flying first class to the fancy resort you have dreamed about and having several weeks to just kick back and enjoy it. What does it feel like? Relaxed, secure, and confident. Feel the emotions and visualize the actions. Feel wealthy to achieve wealth. As you do this, the vibrations you give off into the universe will reflect this. Others will feel that you are wealthy, and people will begin to treat you differently.

If someone is living paycheck to paycheck, the energy they express is that of fear—the fear of losing their job, of being unable to pay rent, and failing to support their family. Employers can pick up on this energy, either consciously or unconsciously, and use it to their advantage by threatening to fire the worker. However, if the worker feels wealthy, even if they have not yet achieved the wealth, their energy will be that of relaxed confidence. If customers feel your desperation when you need to make a sale to save your job, they will flee. Perhaps your goal is to be a sales VP in your current company. Imagine what it will be like to lead a team of 10 direct reports, who each have 100 subordinates beneath them. Visualize yourself in meetings leading the team and consider how it would feel to be in charge and responsible for so many lives.

Feeling the present as well as the future in your grasp is the turbo-powered path to achieving your goals. If you can feel that sensation, and if you can do it often, you will give off the appearance of someone wealthy. Visualize, feel, then achieve.

It is important to note that the path to your goal is never a straight line and unexpected things will happen along the way. Everything happens for a good reason, and everything that happens leads us closer to our goal even though, in the short term, it might not seem that way. You become what you visualize and feel. Don't obsess over the idea that there is a predetermined path that you must follow. Visualize your desired end result and let the path unfold on its own. Undoubtedly, the path will take unexpected detours and it may appear at times that you are going backward. A step back will eventually take you two steps forward, and this can also be a good learning experience.

Let's imagine a scenario where you are forced to take a step back. Getting fired would be interpreted by most as being a seriously negative experience. However, years later when you look back on the event, it may have been one of the best things that happened to your career. Perhaps you landed in a much better job, or it led you to start your own company. I have been around people who interpret every occurrence in their life from a negative point of view. These people are often frustrated and don't achieve much success.

There is an ancient Taoist story about an old farmer. One day, the farmer's horse ran away. Upon hearing the news, his neighbors came to visit. "Such horrible luck," they said. "Maybe," the farmer replied. The next morning the horse returned, bringing with it three other wild horses. "How wonderful," the neighbors exclaimed. "Maybe," replied the old man. The following day, his son tried to ride one of the untamed horses, was thrown, and broke his leg. The neighbors arrived once again to offer their sympathy. "Misfortune has befallen your family!" they exclaimed. Once again, they were only met with another stoic "maybe" from the farmer. The day after, military officials came to the village to draft young men into the army. Seeing the farmer's son's leg broken, they passed him by.

The lesson from the story is to stay positive and look for the good in events as they unfold. It is not easy at first, but practicing being non-judgmental and avoiding negative reactions allows us to see the opportunities that arise. A new door cannot open until the old one is closed.

Use the present tense when you talk to yourself in your head. Don't say, "I want to be wealthy." Use terms as if the goal is already achieved—try saying, "I am wealthy." Another trick is to thank the universe in advance for helping you achieve your goals. For example, instead of thinking, "I want to become wealthy" or "I want to achieve 150 percent of my target this year," you can think, "Thank you for making me wealthy." Or "Thank you for allowing me to achieve 150 percent." When you thank the universe in advance, you'll be surprised at how much closer you are to achieving your goals.

You can be creative with your intentions: they can be a blend of personal and career. Every improvement you achieve in your personal life will assist your work life, and vice versa. How does improving my free throws help my sales management? If you have a personal goal to get into better shape, then the extra energy you get from being in shape will help you at work. If you have a hard-driving boss who piles on the stress, you may have this goal: "When my boss gets angry, I will not internalize the stress and I will resolve the issue without getting emotional." This is a goal that will carry over to your personal life and improve it. The more we can remove the fears that hold us back, the better workers, leaders, husbands, wives, parents, and friends we become.

ACTIVITY

At night, before bed, sit in a quiet place, and visualize your goals in your mind.

Think about all that the good things you want coming into your life, and all the bad things you wish would just leave.

You can also do this as you lie in bed at night.

The few moments you have before you slip into sleep are a good opportunity to program your goals.

REVENGE & KARMA

To come to a true understanding of the Earth element, we must also understand the roles of revenge and karma. It is important to let go of unnecessary negativity and burdens if you wish to ground yourself, which is why we discuss letting go of the idea of revenge and properly understanding karma instead.

Contrary to what many believe, karma and revenge are not the same thing—they aren't even similar. Revenge is the act of wishing harm on someone that we think has treated us unfairly. Karma is a cosmic law that operates automatically to reflect our actions on us. I love Frank Sinatra's famous quote: "The best revenge is massive success." Any energy spent thinking about revenge is energy not spent on achieving success. Energy focused on revenge generates negativity and darkness. Perhaps someone insults you, doubts your abilities, or cheats you. Do not wish others ill will, even if you think you were wronged. It is best to just let it go, keep your positive mind, and take Sinatra's advice to focus on massive success.

It is fine to use challenges or negativity from others as motivation. Michael Jordan, considered by many as the best basketball player ever, continually used even the tiniest perceived slight as motivation. The best sports managers are great at using disparaging quotes from opposing players or managers as a rallying cry to motivate their team. As sales leaders, we can do the same thing with our competition. If competitors make unfair claims that their solution is better than yours or that they will pass you in market size, use those comments to light a fire in your team to fight back and win. "Are we going to let XYZ Company walk into our market and try to take our market share? Heck no!" Disparaging comments from competitors can be used to galvanize teamwork and get everyone fired up as one unit.

Every action or thought carries karma, and each action has a ripple effect on society, just as a stone dropped into a calm pond causes waves to ripple out. For example, if a sales manager is ruthlessly bullying an underperforming sales rep, the sad-sack rep will go home in a frustrated mood, which will then affect his interactions at home. He or she may start to quarrel with their spouse in front of the children. The kids will pick up on this, think this is what normal interactions should be like, and later their marriages could very well mirror those of their parents. The stress level in the family will be high. With the additional stress in the workplace and home, the worker will probably have a lower chance of sales success due to the bullying from his boss. As leaders, we need to be aware of how our actions can have a detrimental effect on someone's entire life.

Early on in my sales management career, I had a sales rep who could not admit a mistake and quickly started blaming everyone else for problems that arose on his deals. He fought with our implementation manager. He fought with our billing team. He fought with everyone. After a few months, he had no support and when he ran into an urgent issue with a customer, no one had his back or supported him. His results suffered and he soon left the company. This incident shows us how the feelings we send out into the universe eventually come back to us as karma.

There are times when we, as leaders, must be tough—for example, when we wish to show that we are not satisfied with a subordinate's performance. However, some leaders, especially in the sales area, use anger or bullying as their default mode, which gets tiring for everyone involved. Management achieved with too much fear or bullying has its own consequences. If you are a leader who constantly threatens to fire an employee if they do not meet their target or quota, then you are doing more harm for yourself in the long-term. That employee is only going to develop a negative attitude towards you, and his or her performance may decline even further. They may even walk out and join your competitor, which is detrimental for the company and for your reputation as a sales leader. Your negative actions will come back in the form of karma to hurt your position, and disturb your connection to the Earth element.

REMOVE LIMITATIONS

Fear and stress are often the major factors in thwarting career success. Silicon Valley giant Andy Grove entitled his autobiography *Only the Paranoid Survive*, which is very good advice for anyone who aims to play the game at a high level. Being "paranoid" means to be fully alert to the risks from competitors and poor decision-making. In any leadership role, there is a 100 percent chance that problems and obstacles will occur. The bigger the job, the bigger the problems one needs to be able to resolve.

While being "paranoid" is crucial for success, paranoia is usually associated with a high level of stress, which can take us away from satisfying work and personal lives. How does one stay energized and alert in order to achieve success in the competitive sales world, but simultaneously avoid internalizing any stress? Can it be done? How can we achieve these seemingly opposite, yet critical, goals?

Early on in my career, I was lucky to work with one executive who was at the top of a sales organization of more than 170,000 people globally reporting up to him. One day, I was stressed out about a small issue with a bad-tempered customer. At the same time, I watched as a few different major problems were handled by this exec, some of which came from customers that had claims in the millions of dollars. By the time the problems came to him, they had already escalated up the chain of command and had become highly critical issues. As I watched this exec tackle these problems one by one, I realized he did not internalize the stress—in fact, he didn't let it affect him at all. He was totally calm and grounded. I realized that if I was ever going to become a senior executive, I would need to do the same. I would have to resolve larger and larger problems while, at the same time, not internalizing any of the stress they cause. Sometimes we find ourselves lying awake at night worrying that something might happen, which is counterproductive. We need to remember that more than 90 percent of things we worry about never even happen!

How to Deal with Problems Without Internalizing Stress:

- Calmly assess the situation and be aware of your body. Recognize that the issue lies outside your physical body and not in your gut, shoulders, neck, etc.

- When a stressful situation arises, know that there is an answer and you will eventually find it.

- Focus on what you can control. Understand, but don't worry about, about what is outside your control.

- Analyze the situation and identify people who can help find the answer. Get them involved.

- When subordinates come to you with a problem, have them come up with at least two possible resolutions as well.

- Focus on your objective, your desired result. Then visualize the problem already resolved and you will soon find that your obstacles are not really obstacles.

Fear is another factor that thwarts career success and keeps you from being grounded. When fear is in our heads, there is no room for breakout ideas or solutions to appear. Sometimes thoughts run wild with fear. "If I don't close these two deals, I could lose my job. And if I lose my job, I won't be able to pay my bills." The fear becomes the focus, and the mantra of "How will I pay my bills?" is echoing in your head over and over again. There are two choices that you have when it comes to dealing with fear:

1. **Upgrade your fears and make them stronger.**
2. **Downgrade them and make them weaker.**

Fear is a physical and emotional state of being. To reduce fear and connect with the Earth element, we need to learn how to manage our emotions and keep our body and muscles relaxed. Be aware that fear and anxiety follow certain patterns and learned behaviors. Do you have particular habits you revert to when you are dealing with fear?

To overcome your fears and anxiety, you must start to break up and interrupt these patterns. Unfortunately, negativity is not only prevalent in society, but it is also hard-wired into our system and needs to be unlearned. Our ancient ancestors were constantly in survival mode and needed to be on the lookout for anything that could put their lives in danger. Shelter and safety from adversaries and predators took priority over enjoying a beautiful sunset. We are always committed to overcoming the negative events in our day-to-day lives.

If you want to overcome your fears, turn the tables and welcome them, instead of avoiding them. Deal with them and get them behind you. Anytime you notice the fear popping back up, instead of getting angry at yourself, just notice the sensation and let it float away. Don't internalize it. Don't let the stress go to your neck, shoulders, or stomach. Through meditation, you can learn to release the stress you have consciously and unconsciously acquired over days and decades. As you release the stress, you untangle the tight muscles in your shoulders, stomach, and whole body. Your digestion becomes better. You even start to sleep better! This is what it means to be connected to the Earth element, and truly grounded.

"SUCCESS IS TO BE MEASURED NOT SO MUCH BY THE POSITION THAT ONE HAS REACHED IN LIFE AS BY THE OBSTACLES WHICH HE HAS OVERCOME."

BOOKER T. WASHINGTON

FULL MOON, NEW MOON INTENTION

In this final Earth section, I will leave you with an exercise that can help you connect with yourself and connect with the planet you live on.

One way to get into harmony with the universe while, at the same time, clarifying your intentions is to use the full moon and new moon intention exercise. The moon has a huge impact on each of us and our energy, and its cycle lasts 28 days. The moon causes the ebb and flow of the tides. The moon has even been shown to affect our moods and sleep patterns, although the scientific data on this phenomenon is still a bit inconclusive. Even so, you can still use the moon cycles as a figurative measure for starting anew each month. As humans, we have naturally decided to divide our weeks into seven days, with four weeks fitting perfectly with the moon's cycle.

The full moon presents a time of completion. It is a time for removal, to overcome obstacles, and to relinquish bad habits. It is a time of clearing. On the full moon, decide on the top 10 things you want to have leave your life and make a list. One or two days later, you can get rid of the list to make sure those things leave your life. You can rip up the paper and throw it away. You can make a ceremony and burn the paper each cycle if you want.

The new moon is associated with beginnings and growth. If you want to bring new things into your life or to start a new project, the new moon phase presents a strong foundation on which to begin. On the new moon, decide on your top 10 wishes or intentions, and make a list of every good thing you hope will come into your life. Be as specific as possible. In your mind, pretend that all these good things have already happened, and be grateful for them. Just thinking about them and writing them down has already started the process. We must be open minded about how the universe delivers what we wish for. It will not arrive exactly in the way we expected. But with belief, our intention—once released to the universe—will manifest.

Note: Keep the new moon items to come into your life.

CHAPTER 3

FIRE BOOK

"EVERYONE HAS THE FIRE, BUT THE CHAMPIONS KNOW WHEN TO IGNITE THE SPARK."

AMIT RAY

FIRE BOOK

"The spirit of fire is fierce, whether the fire be small or big; and so it is with battles. The Way of battles is the same for man-to-man fights and for 10,000 a side battles. You must appreciate that spirit can become big or small. What is big is easy to perceive: what is small is difficult to perceive. In short, it is difficult for large numbers of men to change position, so their movements can be easily predicted. An individual can easily change his mind, so his movements are difficult to predict. The essence of this book is that you must train day and night in order to make quick decisions."
Musashi

Today's battlefield is not an actual battlefield, but it takes place via video calls and digital information. But it requires a similar energy that was mustered among warriors of old. Light a fire under the troops—your team members—and keep them motivated! Motivation is sparked by a deep desire within. It brings your inner warrior to life—driven, fearless, and inspired.

This section teaches:

> 1. Art of handling conflict
> 2. Art of motivating and staying motivated
> 3. Art of selling.

THE ART OF WAR—AND BUSINESS

Naturally, we come to associate the Fire element with conflict and war. Ironically, the supreme purpose of The Art of War is actually to avoid war and fighting. Fighting is the last resort. As Sun Tzu wrote: "In the practical art of war, the best thing of all is to take the enemy's country whole and intact; to shatter and destroy it is not so good. So, too, it is better to recapture an army entire than to destroy it, to capture a regiment, a detachment, or a company entire than to destroy them. Hence to fight and conquer in all your battles is not supreme excellence; supreme excellence consists of breaking the enemy's will to resist without fighting."

The generals who won great battles in history were not the greatest out there. The greatest generals were those who achieved their objectives without fighting and, for the most part, stayed anonymous. The business world is highly competitive, so the higher up the corporate ladder you climb, the higher the stakes will become. Having the ability to identify dangerous situations, unscrupulous people and aggressive competitors with sophisticated tactics is important for survival and success. But it doesn't always mean using Fire to burn and destroy. To avoid wars and conflict, one must be a master in the ways of war and conflict, and this is the essence of the Fire element.

The principles of business and war are the same. We need to motivate workers (troops), lead them in the right direction and outperform the competition. In our work lives, there will be countless conflicts between people such as workers, customers, and vendors. The ability to identify and avoid conflict is a key attribute of elite leadership. The Fire element in the form of conflict results in loss of productivity and success. Unresolved conflict results in a chronic situation that is repeated over and over, which will drain the energy from your teams and pose the risk of having top talent walk out of the door. Fire will burn, but you have to be well aware of what it consumes. Energy spent on internal conflict is the energy that could be spent on beating the competition. Do not hire anyone who displays a tendency for conflict. Analyze any conflict in your office and find the instigators. Work with them to change their habits. If they cannot change, move them out of your team or company.

The same goes for interactions with external stakeholders of your company. Avoid fighting with a competitor's sales staff. Instead of fighting or confronting them, be cordial and friendly while, at the same time, competing fairly—not a fire burning out of control. Who knows? A competitor's rep might want to change jobs, which means they could bring all their know-how and customers to you. Of course, there are times when you just might want to selectively use the power of fire in a conflict with a competitor to get them to lose sight of their strategy and make mistakes.

Warfare is based on deception. If your competitor is quick to anger, you can irritate or entice them into taking irrational actions. But like fire in real life, the Fire element must be managed with care, lest it burn out of control.

DE-ESCALATION: HANDLING CONFLICT AND PROBLEM RESOLUTION

The enlightened leader knows that, in business, conflicts between workers, customers, and vendors are unavoidable and often beyond our control. However, we do have control over our reaction to these conflicts. The ability to identify and resolve these conflicts, and avoid potential conflict before it emerges, is a key attribute of good leadership.

When resolving conflict, most people take one of three options. They overreact, get emotional, or avoid it. In each case, the situation escalates out of control and continues to resurface.

The best approach is to practice the "art of de-escalation," which involves staying calm and quickly lowering the tension level amongst the quarreling parties. This can be like dampening a fire with water or sand. When talking to a colleague or customer who is agitated, do not raise your voice. Stay calm and help the other person calm down before they too resort to yelling. Listen to what the other person wants you to hear; you don't have to agree with it. Be aware of your body language and keep it neutral and non-threatening. Often, just letting the other side share their feelings will cause them to become more cooperative, and many arguments will dissolve.

After listening to their reasoning, find areas that everyone can agree upon. Often, this is the big picture: "We all want the project to be delivered on time to the customer's satisfaction, so now let's review the steps we will take to get there." Think of ideas that can satisfy both sides. Convince both parties to work towards a solution and meet up again to resolve the conflict. If it is an argument that cannot be resolved, both sides can simply "agree to disagree." When the issue is resolved, engage in some sort of ritual to mark your shared success: a handshake or coffee together will provide some sort of closure and will increase communication.

Some conflicts occur when people overstep their boundaries and venture into another's territory. Clear job titles and responsibilities help avoid this. Create a framework for decision making and business practice and make it available for all to see. When you must intervene in a conflict, show that you are striving to do so in a just and decisive fashion. If two employees don't get along, separate them, move their seats, or put them on different projects.

Leaders define what acceptable behavior in an office is. I find it is good to have a near-zero level of tolerance for quarreling in the office. Office fighting zaps the productivity of two or more workers and takes energy away from speaking to customers and other important actions. This might be even more critical when employees return to the office after a forced quarantine, such as in the recent global Covid-19 pandemic. Individuals will likely be on edge, which raises the tension level in the office. Leaders set the tone. Through the art of de-escalation—that is, keeping fires from raging out of control—leaders can improve teamwork and productivity.

THE ART OF HEALTHY CONFLICT

No, the title of this section does not contradict the previous one. The keyword in this section is "healthy" conflict. Conflict can be an engine for creativity and advancement, just as fire was one of early man's most important discoveries. The most substantial technological leaps have occurred during times of war. However, it is crucial to separate healthy conflicts from "unhealthy" ones, which we discussed in the previous section.

Healthy conflicts can encourage different teams and individuals to work harder and climb to the top of the organization. It can light the fire of motivation deep within each team member. Achieving targets or goals to win contests, special bonuses, and president clubs are examples of this. However, if overused, this technique can hurt the spirit of teamwork, especially if one internal team wants to beat another one so badly that they withhold information or leads— an act that is detrimental to the entire company.

Once, I hired a group of eight extremely aggressive and collaborative sales reps, all of whom started work on the same day. They all went to sales boot camp at the same time and developed a close, supportive team with unreal chemistry. On their own, they started a competition to see who would close the first deal amongst them. It was friendly, but some of the reps were very competitive. The youngest of the reps closed the first deal on December 27, and the one whom I saw as the most aggressive closed a deal the very next day. It was interesting to see who the most competitive reps were. For some, they were competing with their teammates to be on top. For others, they were less competitive with their coworkers but more competitive in the marketplace.

Golf provides a similar scenario. In a foursome, some players may be competing against the course to score well, while others are competing against themselves to beat a previous best score. Then there are those who only really care about beating the other three people in the foursome.

Healthy conflicts have a place in driving creativity and can be useful in brainstorming sessions—for example, for marketing strategies or overcoming problems. In creative situations, healthy conflict validates solutions by forcing each member to justify every decision made, and the collective idea is scrutinized to get the best ideas out of the group. Open discussions and debates will lead to better decisions.

I remember being in a management strategy training session at a time when the company I worked for was selling a lot of hardware. However, some people in the company thought we should be focused on selling more professional services. The leadership team was divided in half on the direction the company should take. During this strategy session, we were put into two teams of five people each, and then given 15 minutes to create our cases before starting the debate. After 10 minutes of spirited debate, the trainer abruptly stopped the session and made the teams swap arguments. We were suddenly debating the points from the other side against what we thought was best. It was quite insightful for me to get into the minds of the other team and argue from the opposing point of view. In the end, the exercise helped us as a team look at all the options from all angles. I have used this topic-swapping strategy from time to time, especially if the conversation gets stuck and we need to make a change to find the solution.

Unhealthy conflict in the office is easiest seen when it becomes personal. Saying "You got this all wrong" or "This is your mistake" is the fastest way to increase negative emotions and cause a potential office fight. Avoid making personal statements, which will end up hurting someone's feelings, and disrupt the team and progress of your main missions. Instead of saying, "You said you would do this by this morning," try saying, "The project needs to be finished today. What do we need to do to make that happen?" Avoid starting sentences with "You should" or "You always." Conflict is not a bad thing at times and has its place when utilized correctly, just like the responsible use of fire. Keeping the conflict positive and non-toxic is important.

MOTIVATION

There exists the fire of conflict, and then there exists a fire within each individual who enters the business world. This is the fire of motivation, and you will need to learn how to harness it in order to drive everyone in your team towards maximum productivity. Every sales rep has different hot buttons that motivate them—the fuel for their fire. The top seven motivators are:

1. Autonomy (Leave me alone)
2. Possibility of promotion
3. Special training/mentoring
4. Recognition of achievement
5. Work flexibility/freedom
6. Belief in mission
7. Money

When we learn what motivates and drives each member of the team, we can make sure each member is firing at 100 percent efficiency. Take time to connect with each worker to find out what drives them.

As managers, there are some things we can control and some that we can't. For example, in a large organization, it is difficult to change the corporate culture, but we can control the culture of our team. Don't focus on things that are out of your control. Instead create the culture you want on your team through hiring, training, get-togethers, and more. If there are larger organizational cultural aspects that are detrimental to your team, you can often protect your team from them, which is something they will appreciate.

For the team to be fully motivated, the leader must spell out the direction towards success. You must outline the goals and the core values, and your team has to understand and buy into your vision. If you can find a noble cause that everyone can understand and rally behind, it will be quite powerful. I will once again bring up the example of sports coaches who use fiery speeches and comments from the rival team to fire up their players. Sales leaders can use this strategy with their teams. You can use quotes and questionable tactics from your competitors to motivate your workers.

It is best to find champions on the team who buy into the greater vision and can help bring the rest of the team forward. You must be careful of negative people who don't buy into the vision and try to sabotage it. It only takes one person to destroy momentum. If you have these people on the team, you need to remove them or move them into another role where they cannot negatively affect the team. You could give them an unappealing territory and maybe they will just leave on their own. When the team is motivated, then enthusiasm and success will build. The rush of energy bursts outward like powerful, yet controlled, fire.

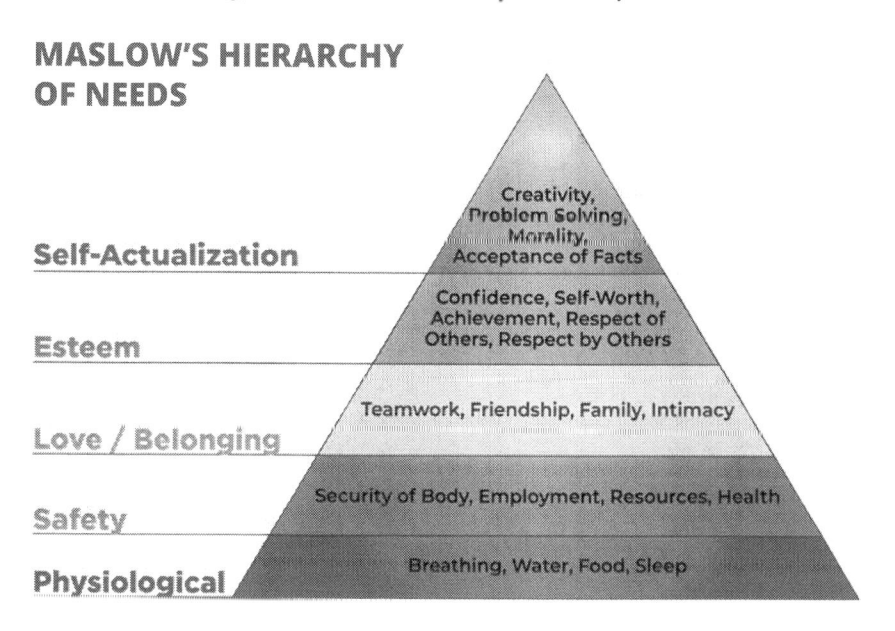

MASLOW'S HIERARCHY OF NEEDS

Self-Actualization — Creativity, Problem Solving, Morality, Acceptance of Facts

Esteem — Confidence, Self-Worth, Achievement, Respect of Others, Respect by Others

Love / Belonging — Teamwork, Friendship, Family, Intimacy

Safety — Security of Body, Employment, Resources, Health

Physiological — Breathing, Water, Food, Sleep

In order to light the fire of motivation inside your team, you need to properly understand their needs. Most readers are aware of Maslow's hierarchy of needs, comprising a five-stage model of human needs.

These are:

> **Physiological needs:** Air, food, shelter, sleep
> **Safety needs:** Security, order, minimal fear
> **Belongingness needs:** Friendship, family, intimacy, trust
> **Esteem needs:** Dignity, achievement, reputation
> **Self-actualization needs:** Self-fulfillment, realizing potential

Recognize that workers are not all motivated in the same way and are at different levels in Maslow's hierarchy. Some people come to work to earn money (existence/physiological needs), some to meet others and be part of a group (belonging needs), and some to earn a promotion (self-esteem needs). Most people are a combination. In a sales setting, motivating sales reps with safety needs can be done by offering good commissions and a friendly working environment. For the sales reps looking for belongingness, show them respect and recognition, and involve them in the team. For those that are growth-oriented, make their work challenging and interesting, and give them stretch goals. For those with self-realization needs, praise them and provide growth opportunities. As a leader, you need to offer different incentives to motivate each rep.

As needs are structured in a hierarchy format, once a lower need has been met, the worker would move up to the next need. For example, a person who is living paycheck to paycheck and in debt will be motivated at the level of the bottom two needs, including food, shelter, and security. They are too busy worrying about surviving in the next month to worry about personal growth or esteem. Sales managers who often threaten their employees with firing will keep the worker from rising above the safety needs. In this scenario, sales reps will be motivated to sell, but will not feel loyalty and will be looking for greener pastures. Sales reps who feel respected and have a sense of achievement and fulfillment with their job will go the extra mile and can create something great for your company. From the teachings of Plato (Western) and Sun Tzu (Eastern), probably the most important common wisdom can be summed up in two words: "Know thyself."

TEAMWORK

Once you have figured out every team member's individual needs, and have figured out what motivates them, the next step is to ignite the fire of *team spirit.*

How many people remember the 2004 US men's Olympic basketball team? The team was built with the greatest players on the planet at that time, including Allen Iverson, Tim Duncan, Carmelo Anthony, Dwyane Wade, and LeBron James. However, they were not prepared. They did not play as a team and, as a result, did not win the gold medal. In fact, they barely beat Lithuania for the bronze. Talent alone sometimes is enough to win, but not always. This team can teach us is that average talent playing together as a team can beat a team of superstars playing individually.

The great NBA coach Phil Jackson used the concept of tribal leadership to measure the progress of his teams. The innovative book *Tribal Leadership* by Dave Logan, John King, and Halee Fischer-Wright lays out the five stages of team development:

Stage 1 — **Life sucks:** Characterized by despair and hostility.
Stage 2 — **My life sucks:** Characterized by apathetic people who perceive themselves as victims and are passively antagonistic.
Stage 3 — **I'm great (and you're not):** Focused primarily on individual achievement and a "lone wolf" culture. Winning is personal and not a team thing.
Stage 4 — **We're great (and they're not):** Dedicated to tribal pride and the belief that "we're great (and they're not)". Teams thrive on having a strong adversary to use as motivation.
Stage 5 — **Life is great:** A rare stage of enlightened teamwork characterized by a sense of wonder.

Think of your current sales team and what words come to mind? Are people supportive? Selfish? Does it seem like people enjoy their jobs or enjoy their lives? How does the team feel? Does it feel heavy? Light? Nauseating? Fun? Understanding the state of the team is important for improvement. Getting contributions from all members is the best and lowers the risk of relying on a few superstars. The best sports teams develop a culture of winning and have a set process and clear direction for success. When one player gets injured, another can step in and fill the role seamlessly. As an analogy, imagine that one sales rep on your team goes on holiday or is out on training. If there is a team mentality, then a colleague will gladly cover their accounts while they are out and be experienced enough to do things right.

Bringing any team—sales or sports—to Stage 5 is extremely rare. Choose your team members wisely. Avoid people who cause trouble or turmoil. Replace those who don't fit. It is hard to move past Stage 4 because it takes a lot of time and attention.

CHARACTERISTICS OF SUCCESSFUL SALES MANAGERS

If you ask someone to visualize a typical successful sales manager in a competitive industry, many people instantly think of the overly aggressive driver who pressures their team using threats such as, "If you miss your sales quota, you will be fired!" That's a lot of stick and a very little carrot, and poor use of the Fire element. These words will indeed motivate sales reps to work harder, but is it the best route that can be taken? The reps will resent this treatment and could develop a negative attitude, which can become contagious in an office. The spirit of teamwork and collaboration can be damaged, leaving you vulnerable if your top reps walk out. Recall the most rewarding moment you've had in your business career. You're probably thinking of the time you took part in a great team, which cooperated and worked together in harmony to achieve something special. And at the forefront of this amalgamation of talent there likely stood a mindful leader.

The ultimate goal of your job is to get yourself and your subordinates working at maximum productivity by creating an atmosphere of teamwork and fair play. Yelling and threatening might be the simplest way to manage sales reps, but it is better to earn the respect of the team by displaying a balanced and measured demeanor. This is a big part of what mindful sales leadership is all about.

"FOR THE STRENGTH OF THE PACK IS THE WOLF, AND THE STRENGTH OF THE WOLF IS THE PACK."

RUDYARD KIPLING, *THE JUNGLE BOOK*

History is full of examples of enlightened leadership—leaders whom people trust 100 percent and would get behind whatever he or she proposed. These leaders range from Alexander the Great to John Wooden, the famed UCLA basketball coach. They inspire loyalty, and you might often hear their followers state: "I would do anything for that man" (or woman, as the case may be). In the upper ranks of senior management, the best leaders are the ones who treat everyone fairly regardless of their title or status. And the worst leaders are the ones who treat "the little people" poorly. I find myself cringing at people who treat their waiter, or anyone they consider "beneath them" poorly. Being a server is a hard job to begin with—there is no reason to be nasty to people in these kinds of challenging positions.

As managers, it is important to "know your staff"—know them on a human and personal level. A direct report is a direct report, but never forget that he or she is also a human being. Everyone is motivated by different factors and all reps have different needs. Listen to the team and every individual in it about what is bothering them. Coach them. Be interested. If they come to you with work problems, ask them to have two ideas for potential solutions. Make them think and learn to problem-solve. Lead from the front. Establish a reputation as the hardest-working person on the team. If subordinates think you are hardworking and caring, they are much more willing to put in the extra hours to kick ass. The best managers have had experience as a rep in the field, so use that experience to relate to your team. It can help create one of the most critical aspects of success—team bonding. A strong team bond is greater than any individual.

Part of building that bond is to NOT continually single out individuals—either heaping praise on the top sales rep or denigrating the lowest-performing rep. Find ways to encourage each team member, and always look for good points for each rep.

The ability to bring people together is becoming more valuable than ever. Not just uniting the sales team, but being able to knock down silos and increase collaboration throughout an organization—specifically with sales and all the other teams that sales interact with. Sales leaders who can foster a collaborative culture with marketing, operations, legal, and others set their teams up for greater success. Getting people who don't report to you to cooperate and collaborate is a sign of real leadership. Rare is the politician who can consistently reach across the aisle and cooperate with those holding different views.

When it comes to leadership and management, many erroneously believe they are the same. People with great leadership capabilities are inspirational, charismatic, and convey big ideas. Good managers are pragmatic and get things done. Good managers have the foresight and have a good grasp on the current situation in a company. Good leaders have a vision and can always see the correct direction. Managers maintain leaders' development. Managers are good at tasks and compliance, while leaders focus on people and empowering them. Managers rely on their title and control their subordinates, while leaders build trust and use it to influence others. Many senior executives have both skills. It is good to understand both so we can be aware and develop both skill sets.

The best sales leaders can light fires under their team by "create a sense of urgency" to achieve goals without threats of firing or negativity. Showing the market potential opportunities, threats from competitors and windows of opportunity are more positive ways to get reps motivated. Healthy internal competitions can also be useful. As much as possible, leaders should choose actions that create positive ripples. When we choose actions that bring contentment and success to others, the fruit of our karma is the same.

Each company has its own corporate culture. Is your current company one of teamwork and collaboration? Do you enjoy coming to work every morning? I am lucky to work for a company that has a great corporate culture—at the macro level at our headquarters in San Jose, and at the micro level in the Japan office. Life is too short to work for a company where you dread Monday mornings and are not satisfied with the workplace. If you find yourself in a job or company that is not fun or satisfying, it is time for a change.

SELLING

Now that we have discussed conflict and motivation, we must discuss the fiery and driven world of **sales**. This field is fast-paced and requires a sincere amount of passion, drive, and motivation, which is why it is included within the Fire section. Sales are all about connecting with customers, developing an understanding of their problems (or "hot buttons"), and delivering a solution to fix those problems.

The best reps pay full attention to customers—not just their words but their body language and all other signs. Be quiet and listen to the customer, then repeat back what was just said to show you understand. Reps should always take notes to show they are proactively listening. Customers must feel secure and trust the rep before they transfer their wealth for a purchase.

It's important to look for a common topic with the customer before the "selling" starts. Maybe they have a University of Michigan iPhone cover. Maybe there is a picture on the wall of them sailing. Find out what the customer is interested in, ask them about it, and get them talking. Be interested and show them that you are interested in them. Everyone likes talking about themselves. Do your research ahead of time. I had one very important interview and I found the guy on Facebook where I learned that he loves to restore cars. During the first 10 minutes of the interview, he passionately spoke about a recent car he had just fixed up. It put him in a great mood once we started discussing my employment, which ultimately proved positive. Just as importantly, take time to understand the customer's business and industry, and how your solution could potentially be of benefit before the first meeting. Checking recent press releases is a good place to start.

With appropriate nods and genuine smiles, you are showing the customer that you understand, agree, and are listening to their opinions— kindling the fire of sympathy and understanding. The best impressions are made when you stop talking about yourself so you can focus on them. Ask more questions than you answer. I've found that the key to a lasting first impression is to discuss a topic that you both care about, ask insightful questions to better understand their point of view, and then provide a new perspective on their thinking based on your own experiences. This not only shows the person that you're listening to but also provides them with lasting value. You need to be relaxed and look like you know what you are talking about. At the end of the day, the best way to achieve that is to be yourself. Your instinct knows better. You need to know that:

- If customers feel pressured by you, the answer is no.
- If customers feel like you're trying too hard to be liked, the answer is no.
- If customers don't think you understand their business, the answer is no.
- If customers don't understand what you're saying, the answer is no.

To be most effective in sales today, it's imperative to drop your "sales" mentality and act as if you've already closed the deal. When you do this, it shifts your relationship with the customer to a whole new level. This is what we call the assumptive sales technique. When discussing the deal, you assume that the customer has already said yes, and this relays your confidence and professionalism to the customer. But it is important not to get too ahead of yourself and come off as rude or stubborn. Just as the fire of unnecessary conflict can damage teams, the fire of being overly pushy can damage the relationship with the customer.

Selling often carries negative connotations, but sales is essentially about problem-solving and creating value for people. People pay for value. "You can have everything in life you want if you just help enough others get what they want," stated sales legend Zig Ziglar. Learn to add even more value. If you have a meeting or an important phone call ahead of you today, take a deep breath before you start it. Visualize your goal for the meeting. As it starts, focus your intent on what your prospect or partner is about to say to you while being mindful. Know thy customer.

ACCOUNTABILITY IN SALES

Deception is used by everyone. Surprise parties can't happen if deception is not involved. If your boss's boss has an idiotic idea and asks for your advice, it is best you filter your reply, or you may soon be looking for a new employer. One mustn't go out in the business world practicing deception in a wicked manner. But you must understand different deception strategies and tactics in order to spot when others are trying to take advantage of you. Anyone involved in contract negation knows this well; being able to counter deception can save you lots of money and aggravation.

I recently read about a hotel chain CEO who shows up at his hotels unannounced so he can check the real quality of the hotel's service as a regular customer. If the staff had been given a heads up that the CEO was coming, he would have gotten the VIP treatment. I once had an interview at Apple and the most senior person in the room pretended to be a part of admin support. It wasn't until a week later I found out they were actually the head of HR for the entire Asia–Pacific region.

"All warfare is based on deception. Hence, when we are able to attack, we must seem unable; when using our forces, we must appear inactive; when we are near, we must make the enemy believe we are far away; when far away, we must make him believe we are near."
San Tzu, *The Art of War*

COMPETITION

1. External Competition
Sales is a game, but a very serious game. We need our jobs to provide shelter and food for our families and loved ones. But our direct competitors are trying to take away our livelihood! We must face our competition with the idea of total domination. Good, honest, and fair competition—yet we must give impassioned, 100 percent effort in our desire to win. Study the competition. Avoid their strengths and strike at their weaknesses. Understand where you are superior. In *The Art of War*, there are five essentials for victory:

> - He will win who knows when to fight and when not to fight.
> - He will win who knows how to handle both superior and inferior forces.
> - He will win whose army is animated by the same spirit throughout all its ranks.
> - He will win who, prepared himself, waits to take the enemy unprepared.
> - He will win who has military capacity and is not interfered with by the sovereign.

As a sales leader, it is never good to show the team you are fully satisfied with their performance. You need to keep their flame of motivation burning. Even when your team is doing great, there is always room for improvement. I have seen this with the best managers at all levels of sports and in all major leagues—from Pep Guardiola at Manchester City to Bill Belichick of the New England Patriots. When their teams are winning, they don't ease up on their opponents or their players. In victory, they will say, "We played well today but there are several areas we can improve upon." Complacency is the first step in creating a losing culture.

Always respect your opponent and competitor and show some humility. But you can still fire up your team by explaining that competitors are trying to take their lunch, and their teammate's lunch—because that is what is happening. If a competitor disparages your team or company, use that to motivate your team. Print out the article and hang it on the wall or forward it to your staff.

Always keep the energy level high within your team. The best thing about people who aim for the very best is that they often get it. Demand the best from your people and drive them to reach their potential. Support them, mentor them, and they will follow you anywhere.

2. Healthy Internal Competition

We not only have competition with our direct competitors but also competition amongst our own sales staff. Unhealthy competition amongst a team is poison. When team members are looking out only for themselves, you end up with a selfish team in which none of the members views their success within the context of the group. When colleagues begin snatching leads from one another and not supporting each other, unhealthy competition sets in. Getting your sales team to work as a cooperative unit is imperative. Internal conflicts—fires burning out of control—waste energy that could have been used for customer acquisition.

Salespeople who understand healthy competition will challenge themselves, but not at the expense of others. A very effective tactic is to pair new employees with more experienced sales reps so they can learn from experience and learn to overcome conflict. You can also create competitions that internal teams can win. It is best to have more than one winning team, and more than one winner. Recognize the sales reps who are doing well and reinforce their strong performance. Have the successful reps run sales training to share what they have done to achieve success. When colleagues cheer for each other and support one another's progress, everyone wins—especially your company.

SALES PROCESS

Your team must have a rock-solid sales process that everyone uses, or else you are leaking revenue and efficiencies. There is not a one-size-fits-all process for the wide variety of sales situations. For example, someone who is selling a used 747 airplane will have a very different process and set of sales tools than a person selling memberships at a local gym. However, having a set structure to follow when making a sale is important. I have interviewed hundreds of sales reps over the last several years. I always ask if they have a process that they follow, and from which employer they learned this process. I was surprised at the number of large brand name companies that don't have any standard process to drive the efficiency of their sales.

A company needs to take into account customer pain, who the decision-maker is, and what value you can offer customers. For IT sales, I find the biggest problem for lost sales is not identifying and getting buy-in from the key decision-maker or economic buyer.

CHAPTER 4

WATER BOOK

"BE FORMLESS, SHAPELESS LIKE WATER. NOW YOU PUT WATER INTO A CUP, IT BECOMES THE CUP. YOU PUT WATER INTO A BOTTLE, IT BECOMES THE BOTTLE. PUT IT IN A TEAPOT, IT BECOMES THE TEAPOT. WATER CAN FLOW, WATER CAN CRASH—BE WATER, MY FRIEND."

BRUCE LEE

WATER BOOK

Accepting and understanding change while staying clear and balanced is crucial. Today's business world and society are changing faster than ever, which requires that you change your skill set in order to succeed. In evolution, it is not the strongest of species that survives, it's the one that adapts. In the Earth book, we discussed how we can ground ourselves and remain balanced, whereas in the Fire book we discussed how we can remain motivated in times of conflict. Within the Water section, we discuss how you can adapt to change. Communication is a critical factor that is included in the Water book because words are the driving force for change. Language is seemingly harmless, but true water spirits know that it is an incredibly powerful tool to bring about change—it is up to you whether you use communication for negative or positive effects in your life. This section teaches:

1. Adaptability in a quickly changing world and market
2. Adaptability through communication

"With water as the basis, the spirit becomes like water. Water adopts the shape of its receptacle; it is sometimes a trickle and sometimes a wild sea."
Musashi

ACTIVITY

Take 15 seconds to quickly review from memory the words you use in your head, especially when you are in stressful situations.

As you pass through the next few days, become aware of how you speak to yourself.

If you catch yourself being harsh to yourself, then you need to start being nicer and having a more positive inner dialogue.

If you make a mistake, don't beat yourself up. Just say, "This is a learning experience" and forget about the mistake.

When you catch yourself treating yourself harshly, notice it, make a positive change, and just let the old thought float away.

Talk to yourself as if you are talking to someone you love.

Talk to yourself like you are trying to impress some sophisticated and sharp people.

Hold yourself to a high standard when it comes to your inner dialogue.

THE ART OF COMMUNICATION

Water has a hidden power. It prefers to lay calm on most days, gently lapping at the shores and remaining a background presence in everyone's lives. But when the storms arrive, water becomes a force to be reckoned with, rising over us and drowning entire cities before our eyes. Similarly, the words we speak may not seem that important to us on most days. Like water that surrounds us in so many forms, language is something we've grown so used to—we are not even aware of what a powerful tool it can be. Mindful leaders must have a strict grasp over language and the art of communication. They can wield it on most days like a gentle ocean wave, using it to encourage teammates and pass compliments on their hard work. Or they can use it as an ocean torrent, letting it flood over the listener so that a highly impactful statement is imparted.

1. Internal Dialogue

We all talk to ourselves in our heads. When you talk to yourself, how do you treat yourself? Are you friendly and supportive? If your inner voice says, "I am so stupid" or "I always make mistakes," then you will find it hard to move past the negative mindset. Inner dialogue is the conversation our ego has with itself. There is no separation between inner dialogue and what manifests in your life: the words you repeat over and over in your head ultimately set the path for your future to follow.

Some people's internal dialogue is so harsh, if they treated their colleagues or subordinates with the same tone and words, it would be legal grounds for abuse. Some people do let their internal dialogue slip out into the external world. We have all heard people who verbally chastise themselves when they think they did something wrong: "John, you bonehead!"

Negative thoughts never create a positive life. When we have a positive, uplifting, and optimistic internal dialogue, good things are attracted to our careers and lives. Don't keep a negative loop playing in your head, drowning out the potential for positivity. You spend more time with yourself than anyone else: give yourself something good to listen to!

2. Communicating with Others

I once worked for a company where the senior management used the terms "push back" and "fight" to get things done internally. Workers who "pushed back" were praised. The internal corporate culture was very adversarial between departments and stress was high. Once I was instructed, "You need to push back and fight with Derek to get him to agree with our stance." I replied, "Why don't I just discuss this with Derek, get him to see the benefits, and get his buy-in without any conflict?" I changed my actions from that day and built many internal allies, eventually getting a lot more accomplished.

The way you act as the leader sets the tone for the rest of the team. The words you use are very important. Use the power of the Water element as you adapt, removing negative and adversarial words from your team environment. Use words such as collaboration and teamwork. Be friendly. Terms such as "cooperate," "teaming," "teamwork," "confident," and "smart" can help. When people have positive topics to discuss, praise them. When people are negative or they waste time gossiping, then keep your distance from them.

It takes two people to fight. If you as a leader or worker don't fight, then the other side is just swinging in the wind. Some workers only know how to fight. When you don't fight with them, you are operating on your territory and not where they are comfortable.

One way to make your team feel inclusive is to use the word "We," and not "I." "We" is inclusive and makes everyone feel included. I had one manager start seven sentences in a row with the words "I want." It was a constant stream of "I want the team to sell this. I want the team to do that." And his very last sentence was, "And I want you to help me achieve this." Looking around the room, the engagement and motivational level of the staff was extremely low. Many sales managers use terms like "my team," or worse, "my people." When you create a strategy, make people feel that their voices are being heard. Start your sentences with "we" and be inclusive towards your team.

Our thoughts create our reality. The thoughts and messages we send to our subordinates and sales teams also matter. There are no companies that are without fault or problems. We have all been in companies where people constantly complain about the company or the boss. If we put our focus on these problems and verbally reinforce them with our peers and subordinates, then the hill we need to climb for success gets steeper. It is like polluting water that was once pristine and clear.

This is especially true of management. Our word and mood trickle down through the organization like water going through cracks in a wall. We don't ignore problems. We address areas that need improvement to make our jobs easier and increase the percentage of success. We focus on the solutions and the positives. If we are in sales, we focus on how we will beat the competitors or what the customer's needs are. Often, it can be just one employee who can wreck the harmony of an office. I have seen some workers who spend more than 50 percent of their time complaining and gossiping. This lowers productivity and morale and acts as a poison to your firm's success. Weed these people out and steer them towards the door if they cannot change themselves.

Good leaders also take time to listen to the people reporting to them. They have balance, and that characteristic gets transferred to the team. When there are big wins, they don't let the team get too high. When a big deal is lost, they don't let the team get low. Like water, they change and adapt to the situation and vessel as needed.

No one likes a pushy salesperson who talks too much. Use your questions to lead the customer where you want them to go. Don't push. Follow the energy and follow the flow. The same applies to your employees. Schedule one-on-one time often. Find out what they are passionate about inside and outside the company. Just listening will make them feel good. Many times, I have had employees come to me with personal or work problems. Just listening to them resolved more than half of the issues. Often people just want someone to listen to them, to care. Then they feel better and can move on. At the end of every conversation with an employee or customer, ask them, "Do you have any requests for me?" or "Is there anything I can do for you?"

In keeping with the careful use of the Water element, monitor your words and thoughts, and don't make a fool of yourself. Don't talk about yourself, talk about others. Don't promise anything you cannot deliver. Don't agree to things you don't want to do and might not follow up on. Don't show off, and don't boast. Don't exaggerate. Stay to what is real and what you can deliver. Become verbally disciplined. Your word is the law. Your credibility and reputation are on the line.

GOSSIP AND CONFIDENTIALITY

Gossip and complaining are one form of communication that sap energy and productivity in the office. As a leader, you need to set the tone for the team. Don't engage in complaining, gossip, or time-wasting chatter. Remain quiet, like a pool of water that is free of waves. Professionally go about your business. Complainers don't want a solution. They just create a habit of negativity and want to recruit others to join in.

Stay tightlipped in the office. Being known as a blabbermouth in the office is a quick way to detour off the fast track. Senior executives can keep secrets and share with others on a need-only basis. Avoid discussions about other workers' personal lives. You don't always need to fill the silence up with chatter—sometimes it is better to stay in comfortable silence. Do not blurt out information on who will be promoted or fired. When senior people share information with you, keep it to yourself. If you get a reputation as a gossiper, you will lose the trust of senior executives and your access to inside information on key issues will be lost. If you show that you can keep a secret, seniors will share insight into what is happening inside and around the company. Knowledge is power, so keep your ears open and mouth closed.

THE ART OF AVOIDING ARGUMENTS

In Dale Carnegie's classic book *How to Win Friends and Influence People*, he writes: "You can't win an argument. You can't because if you lose it, you lose it; and if you win it, you lose it." Why is that? Suppose you triumph over another person and shoot their argument full of holes and show them they are wrong. The other person will feel defensive and inferior, and probably hasn't changed their position one bit. There is even a chance that you convinced them to hold onto their stance even tighter. Harness the power of the Water element, and recognize the need to adapt to situations. Don't create ill will by getting into useless arguments. Know how to pick your battles carefully, and do not contest every position.

If someone says something unfair or attacks you, trying to address each point will lead to a prolonged argument. There are two things you can do instead. Firstly, the quickest and easiest way to end any argument is to simply agree with the other side. A second strategy is to pass the ball back to the other side with a question. "You know, I never thought of it that way. Can you explain it to me a little more?" Often in the second explanation, the antagonist will soften their argument, especially since you haven't argued back to their first attack. Then you can start to look for areas to agree upon and find common ground.

Benjamin Franklin made it a rule never to contradict anyone, which must have greatly reduced potential conflict. He wrote: "I never use language that imparted a fixed opinion, such as certainly, undoubtedly, etc. and I adopted, instead of them, I conceive, I apprehend, or I imagine a thing to be so or so, or it so appears to me at present." When correcting another's a mistake, write something like "it appears your facts might not be correct." This way, if the facts turn out to be correct, then your preface "it appears" is your escape. This language is useful when working with clients and deliverables. Most projects or deliverables have a risk of delay. If a client asks when will a project be completed, give yourself some room for flexibility depending on the circumstances. Writing "We expect to complete the project on xx date" is safer than "The project will be completed on this xx date." This gives an edge over the client/customers, providing you with flexibility and the room to adapt that will ultimately help keep clients satisfied.

BALANCE

Whether you win a big deal or lose a big deal, don't lose your balance, and don't let the team lose their balance. If you win a big deal, be satisfied but don't be overly elevated, and do not become cocky. Don't relax, and don't let the team think they can slouch off now that they have won a major deal. The next day, come into work as if it's day one, and you are starting over on the next great conquest.

If you lose a deal, the way you think about yourself should not be affected one bit, and you should be ready and confident to win the next deal. If you lose, don't think, "Oh you're a loser, and nothing is going to change that." Like a steadily flowing river, don't let your spirit dip, and don't let your subordinates see you down, because their energy will follow yours. Assure the team that setbacks are natural, and the chief thing is to focus on the larger goal. Keep everyone focused and moving ahead. Life and business move in cycles. You won't win every deal. It is the deals you lose that teach you the most. Welcome them, learn from them, and reduce them! If you are in a grim situation, rather than fighting it, love the circumstances. Say to yourself, "Thank you universe for these lessons." Turn negative energy into positive energy. When you remove negative energy, your fears are also removed.

Be fair with your sales team and members. If they work hard and efficiently but still lose a deal, don't get angry at them. Make sure you review with the team to understand the areas where everyone could have performed better. If the team missed some basic parts of the deal, such as not identifying the correct decision-maker or available budget, then you probably need to show them you are not happy and perhaps raise your voice or call some members out. Just because you raise your voice does not necessarily mean you raise anger inside of you. You can show your displeasure and even raise your voice, without letting the anger overwhelm you and everyone around you. You can keep your spirit balanced and at a steady level while you handle various situations throughout the day.

Never lose your peace of mind. Don't let people yank your chain. If someone does, keep away from them. Internally investigate: "Why does this person bother me?" Then release the thought to the air and ignore them. Stay away from people who drain your energy. Life is too short to hang out with people who drain you. Most of us are too busy to find time for the people we want to hang with, so don't waste time on the people you don't want to hang with. Don't let your spirit get too high or too low, especially as the leader. Your spirit remains unchanged.

ACTIVITY

Mindful leaders tend to:

- Stay calm and balanced in the mist of chaos
- Set and communicate a clear mission
- Use intuition to hear and feel what is not said and see what is not visible
- Be flexible and receptive to change
- Proactively listen to employees and customer
- Embrace health and balance of the body
- Have very little ego
- Create and achieve seemingly impossible goals
- Reduce conflict to increase efficiencies

FOCUS AND LISTENING (TO CUSTOMERS)

During Bill Clinton's second term as president of the United States, I was lucky to be invited to a speech in Tokyo that he made to about 150 people at the Capitol Hotel Tokyu. The room was packed, and he was the last person seated, directly in front of the stage and podium. There were three speakers scheduled before Clinton; however, as the first speaker started, absolutely no one listened, and the audience gawked at the president.

President Clinton then did something I will never forget. He placed his full and undivided attention on the speaker. Clinton looked at the speaker as if he were about to share the meaning of life. The look on his face was of one of pure fascination and he was completely engaged. He was proactively listening, and he let everyone else know as much. Very soon, the entire audience followed the president's lead and was also focused on the speakers. Clinton did a great service to the speakers with his gracious and thoughtful actions. Since then, I have employed the same tactic thousands of times, whether I am with a customer or hosting an event with speakers. When I am with a customer, I not only listen but let them know I am listening. For example, if I hand off to an engineer to do a demo, I don't start looking at my phone and disengage. I listen to the engineer intently in front of the customer, which encourages the customer to also listen. When the engineer makes a point that benefits the customer, I nod my head approvingly. Often, I see the customer start to nod their head positively in unison. When the customer speaks, I not only listen but proactively listen. I take notes and repeat back what the customer says. If the customer is boring, it is even better. Probably the past five sales reps who met the customer were yawning, disengaged, and ready to end the meeting and leave. I ask questions and stay engaged, which makes the customer happy. This is the power of adaptability that lies at the heart of the Water element.

DO LESS

In an article published in 1963 by the *Harvard Business Review*, Peter Drucker said: "There is surely nothing quite so useless as doing with great efficiency what should not be done at all."

Phil Jackson was famous for not calling timeouts when his team hit poor stretches, which is counter to standard coaching tactics. Asked why he didn't call a timeout when his team was getting hammered in one game, Jackson replied, "I left the team on the court because sometimes they need to figure it out for themselves."

You need your sales reps to learn to resolve issues and close deals on their own. Do not bail them out or make them dependent upon you or others. Doing less will give more "air" and flexibility for your direct reports to take on more responsibility. To get ahead, we instinctively think we need to do more. Often by doing less will we get ahead faster, giving our natural ability to adapt its time to shine.

CHANGE

"Change is the only constant in life" is a famous quote from the Greek philosopher Heraclitus. Maybe you've heard it quoted as, "the only constant in life is change." But the speed of change isn't always constant. In the tech world, where I currently ply my trade, change seems to happen almost daily, with some of those changes being tremendous while others are far more subtle.

If history has taught us anything, it is that times of struggle, such as war and other global catastrophes, bring about the most change. Many parts of the Western world have not any serious existential threats for the past couple of generations, so the Covid-19 pandemic provided a large jolt to society and the workplace. The one thing that will never change is the need for thoughtful corporate leaders who can effectively guide their teams through good times and bad. In short, I believe that the trend of "mindful" management techniques will become more important than ever.

As a general rule of thumb, it is imperative that leaders take care of their own people first. Communication, paired with empathy, is vital. Leaders need to over-communicate and let their teams know that they can reach out with any questions or concerns at any time. It is important that leaders share frequent, clear, and reliable information. Make sure that, in times of crisis, you are quickly sharing new facts that emerge from corporate and government health sources. This idea of sharing information on a regular basis is also important during what most people see as a "normal" business and world environment.

While a crisis brings pain, it also provides the opportunity for self-growth for certain individuals, as well as the chance for (much needed) improvements for humanity. The Water element teaches us that those who can easily adapt to change are the ones who will emerge as winners in the new society that lies beyond the pandemic or any other crisis.

As leaders, change allows us to see opportunities for self-growth and self-care by paying attention to our families and colleagues, as well as other areas for improvement in our personal and professional lives. We need to be able to lead ourselves before we can lead others. Confident self-leadership makes us more authentic and trustworthy, and thus people are more likely to be inspired by us and follow where we lead. The flexible and intelligent leader will understand the negative aspects and risks from the crisis while, at the same time, seizing the opportunity that this crisis presents to develop positive change in ourselves and our teams—all while helping our companies effectively navigate an evolving landscape.

CHAPTER 5

WIND BOOK

"THE WIND BLOWS ON US ALL, BUT IT'S HOW YOU SET YOUR SAIL THAT MAKES THE DIFFERENCE."

JIM ROHN

WIND BOOK

In Musashi's classic, the Wind book included his specific style and strategy when it comes to sword fighting. The broader lesson of the book involves understanding your opponent as quickly as possible. The new era has ushered in shifts in every organization and person's direction. The winds of change are always blowing, and they require constant attention and adjustment, but you must always keep in line with universal principles. We must steer ourselves and our team members in the right direction, help them shed their bad habits and negative assumptions, and help them move closer to building a spirit that is free of doubt and fear. These are the principles of the Wind element, which allows you to understand your opponent and then use this knowledge to bring about improvement in yourself. This section teaches:

1. Understanding of people and power
2. Overcoming obstacles
3. Making friends and practicing humility
4. Mastering the art of hiring and firing

READING PEOPLE

To succeed in the business world, sizing up people quickly is a strong asset.

Musashi wrote, "From one thing, know ten thousand things." Sometimes, you can size up a situation or person very quickly, and it is best if you can do it within an instant. First impressions are extremely crucial. What are your feelings when you first meet someone? Do they seem sad? Confident? Shifty? Do they have downward wrinkles around their mouth showing they have been sad or angry most of their life? Do they have permanent wrinkles in their brow indicating a life full of worry or hardship? Do they seem relaxed and confident? Are they fashionable? If so, perhaps they care more about style over substance.

Perhaps they have one minor trait that you noticed in someone years ago who tried to cheat you on a deal. Perhaps they cannot look you in the eye when answering a key question. Try to quickly size up the situation. Use your eyes, ears, nose, and gut. It is critical to perceive that which cannot be seen. Remember, humans are a part of the animal world—we just had the benefit of evolving more. Animals rely solely on instinct. Until modern times, we were the same. Start to "feel the situation," as quickly as the wind, and you will become more sensitive to an individual's motives and actions. Most people don't fully utilize this ability or are not conscious of it. Having the ability to size up a situation quickly gives you a competitive edge over others in the field.

People are not just made up of their physical bodies. They are also feelings. You need to see those feelings to better understand the people you meet. Know their tendencies and possibilities. Watch their feelings and comprehend them. Do they anger easily? Do they talk about themselves? Are they holding back? See how the feelings and energy flow and allow you to see what will occur in the future.

ACTIVITY

Next time you walk into your workplace or a general social setting, try noting down the different feelings you sense from others.

Make a list of their body language—such as gestures and expressions. In front of each bullet point, add the different emotions each gesture or expression could signify.

For example:

- The person keeps shifting from one foot to another—could signify discomfort, fatigue, nervousness, etc.

"NEARLY ALL MEN CAN STAND ADVERSITY, BUT IF YOU WANT TO TEST A MAN'S CHARACTER, GIVE HIM POWER."

ABRAHAM LINCOLN

ACHIEVING POWER

People who overcome great adversity are revered. However, if someone drops you off in Siberia about 100 kilometers from the nearest town, are you going to lie down and give up or take the challenge and walk? You will walk. Handling adversity is often an instinctive action. Handling power is very different, and often much more difficult.

Many people fail the personality test that comes with gaining power, such as when they become a manager. With any rise in power, it is important to keep your core values intact. Don't take yourself too seriously and keep your ego in check. Keep your feet firmly planted on the ground, as we discussed in the Earth book. Don't start to act differently. Many new managers feel like they need to make sure everyone knows they now have power and start getting "bossy." Their attitude screams, "I am in charge!" New managers must remember how they liked to be treated when they were still the sales rep or subordinate.

One mistake all first-time managers make, at least a few times, is to continue doing things themselves. It takes a little while to shake the "individual contributor" mindset. Managers cannot focus on individual tasks. The Wind element dictates that you should quickly recognize and shed past habits that are counterproductive. In this way, when you move up to the rank of manager, you must focus on helping their team members complete their assignments. Managers need to focus on coaching, supervising, and guiding, not doing the work the salespeople should be doing.

Another area that can cause a new manager difficulty is falling into the despair of "decision paralysis." Managers need to harness the power of the Wind element and make informed decisions quickly. Any delays in decisions can stall the team and entire department from acting and get to their job of selling. *The Art of War* states: "A good decision this week is better than a great decision next week." Time is literally money in sales, and delays can kill a business. If a direct report comes to you with a problem and you are not sure of the answer, ask them: "What do you think we should do?" This will help speed up your decision-making process.

First-time sales managers must learn to effectively "manage up." New managers often forget to update senior folks on progress, issues, wins, and risks. New managers should ask: "How often do you want me to provide the forecast? What format?" They need to show they can operate independently, while at the same time provide their senior management the information they need at the right time.

HIRING, DISCIPLINE, AND FIRING

While it's not a pleasant subject, firing is something that happens in every company. Underperformers on a sales team need to be fired, or your job and the whole organization might be at risk. Keeping below-average sales reps will result in a below-average sales team, which is a danger for your career. Sales organizations are not charities. When staff must let go, it is a stressful situation for all those involved. Showing empathy and compassion in these situations often makes the process quicker and smoother.

I worked for a boss who had made hundreds of workers redundant over his career, and he was very callous and desensitized about the process. Being able to make hasty decisions about firing like this is a prime example of the misuse of the Wind element. Sometimes it would backfire as employees would make complaints to the government labor office, or they would become extremely disruptive.

People being made redundant are most likely under stress in many areas. Embarrassment with their families, financial worries, and losing face with colleagues are all major sources of stress. Showing a little bit of compassion to these workers can go a long way. You can build good will with their colleagues, who also may report to you. Often when one shows kindness, the person is less motivated to fight and will agree to terms easier. It is always best to take action on Fridays, late in the afternoon, when people will go home for the weekend and have time to understand the situation. This also reduces potential office drama with everyone leaving for the weekend.

I worked for a Japanese man who was president in Japan for a large American IT firm. He never wanted anyone to leave, including poor sales staff. Incompetent or underperforming sales staff would have to be moved to another group, such as sales support. The good people left through natural attrition, yet the inferior salespeople stayed. Eventually, results began to suffer, and the president was pushed out the door. The damage to the company was so great that it continued to affect its operations for many years.

Companies follow the laws of evolution–survival of the fittest. If you are not constantly looking for the best talent and evaluating your current talent, then a bigger, faster beast will quickly overpower you. Hiring and working with "A" grade people is great and fun. Getting rid of underachievers is less so. I have seen many leaders become desensitized to the process, forgetting that the individual leaving is human and probably has a lot of stress and personal issues to deal with.

Hiring is the exact opposite—it is a time of excitement. Hiring is the most important thing you will do. An average manager with great staff will overachieve their targets. A great manager with below-average staff will most likely fail. In the interview process, one key area to check is to see if they played team sports. These workers tend to favor collaboration, as it is a critical aspect of a team sport.

Only settle for the very best. Hire people with the drive to win. Check references very carefully, which in the era of LinkedIn is easier than ever.

Human resources used to be called the "personnel department." Nowadays, it feels like workers are just a "headcount" in constant danger of "right-sizing" activities. Make sure your direct reports are adding some value and help them get there. If they cannot add value, they need to leave.

The excellent sales leader constantly keeps their eyes out for A-level talent, and they are constantly recruiting the best of the best. Top leaders are always coaching their staff to continuously improve and motivating them to succeed. Sales are easy—hire the best talent and let them go sell. If you can do this well and get the most productive people on your team, then almost all other difficulties will fall away, and you will have success.

The worst managers are the ones who take a kind of pleasure in firing people. Yes, there are a lot of these people out there. Maybe someone who doesn't fit your team could be good on another team.

In Asia I have, at times, let some top sales performers go, which was a shock to the other members of the team. I had one sales rep in Japan working for me who knew the product better than anyone else and knew all the key people amongst our competitors, but he was lazy and didn't give his work his best effort. On top of that, he would defy requests from his manager (me) and play other political games. I could quickly see that this guy would always cause trouble and it would spread around the team. I let him go to the protest of some of the team members. However, a year later, everyone agreed it was the right decision. Once we had a strong team in place, it was easy to see that we never would have had the harmony we achieved had this troublemaker stayed in the company.

A common business strategy is to "praise in public" and "reprimand in private." One important point: Don't forget to praise. Positive reinforcement goes a long way and creates good morale. Always acknowledge success on the team, sometimes individually and sometimes publicly. However, when it comes to reprimanding, one must sparingly and carefully reprimand in public. Generally, reprimand in private. However, there are times when you need to set an example in front of the whole team or company. I caught a sales rep cheating on his expenses. In this case, I wanted the whole team to know this would not be allowed and that they will be punished if they break the rules.

OBSTACLES

When you are stuck in a situation that you don't want to be in any more, then embrace the element of the Wind, and simply make a change. The definition of insanity is doing the same thing repeatedly and expecting different results. Not changing when stuck will keep you from moving forward. Be flexible. Our time on this planet is limited, and there is nothing you cannot achieve if you follow the way correctly and release your inner passion.

We must accept that obstacles will appear in our path, but we have to fight the impulse to make a mountain out of a molehill. As a leader, if your team runs into a challenge and you walk around the office in a panic, constantly exclaiming, "Oh my God, what a big problem we have!" then the workers will also think that "we have a big problem." The problem instantly becomes more difficult to solve. If the manager portrays the problem as a challenge that can be overcome, then the problem immediately becomes much simpler to resolve. Always keep the team calm and rational.

Challenges and problems are for learning and growth. As the Zen proverb goes: "The obstacle is the path." The difficulty is not designed to derail you, but to help you advance. A positive mindset is essential to accomplish this. Don't let negativity win or it can stop your development. When your desire to overcome is greater than your fears, you'll conquer any obstacles life can throw at you. Eventually, we see the earlier quote change to "The obstacle is temporary." Once I mastered this concept, I learned that "The obstacle is an illusion." This means there is already a solution even before a problem arises. Welcome it, know it will be resolved, resolve it, and learn from it. Then move on, like the wind.

EFFORTLESS SUCCESS

There is a natural flow in the universe that determines how the events in our lives unfold. Most of you have probably felt this power from time to time, even if you were not always conscious of it. For example, in sports, when the game seems to be easy and everything seems to be going right, athletes are considered to be "in the zone." Then there are other days when it feels like nothing is going right, and problems seem to be piling up.

Some believe luck is cyclical, and if one is on a winning streak, inevitably their luck will change. However, by anticipating bad luck, you are inviting it to come over. If you expect bad luck and put out such pessimistic vibes, the universe will always deliver just that. Maybe you have won three large deals in a row. There is no reason you cannot win the next three deals. If you are losing deals, stay positive, analyze what you can improve, and know that bad luck can turn to good luck very quickly. Tough times don't last, but tough (and positive) people do.

You will begin to see that energy and coincidences become coordinated, and things will naturally start to fall into place. Opportunities will start to pop up and, as you are sensitive to the energy around you, you will have an advantage over people who use only their analytical skills. As we saw earlier, Bill Clinton had an amazing ability to feel and sense energy, which he used to connect with people. The vibrations he emitted seemed to resonate with everyone he met. Add that to his great intellect and it is easy to see how he dominated American politics for such a long time.

Don't struggle against the natural flow of the universe. It's like trying to do battle with the wind. If someone or something offends or blocks you, your instant reaction shouldn't be negative. Wait for one minute or just a few seconds and take a breath. The offending person might be surprised that their comments didn't result in an immediate knee-jerk reaction. They might be more open to what you say next and will be more likely to listen to you. You may find that new opportunities pop up that would not have been visible had you reacted in haste.

When something happens to you that you think is negative, just wait, and you will realize the "negative" item has quickly turned positive. Perhaps someone gives you negative criticism. Instead of getting defensive, thank them and don't react too emotionally. If you feel a little hot-headed, wait for the moment to pass and assess the situation.

Think about what the other person said. Perhaps there is some truth in their comment that can make you a better worker or person. What could have been a touchpoint for conflict has become a situation without conflict, and an opportunity for you to improve yourself.

Visualize a natural flow in your life, with everything falling into place right when you need it. Out of that flow, watch your dreams become your reality. In the real world, watch how the energy flows and decide to go with it and not fight it. Perhaps you need to ask your boss for a week off, but she was just told that your team lost a $1 million deal. If you use the power of the Wind element to quickly assess the situation, you might understand that it would be better to wait a couple of hours or even a day before making your request.

I used to be on a global sales call that took place late at night in Japan and I always hated it. The sales leader at headquarters was a fairly nasty man who would attack reports and forecasts that were not perfect, even though nothing is ever perfect in sales. Unfortunately, I was always scheduled to report directly after the director for Australia. Australia always missed its target and lost deals. This would incense the leader at headquarters to no end and put him in a terrible mood, right before it was my time to give an update. Entering the forecast call with a tyrant who was just put in a horrible mood was something I dreaded each week. I tried like crazy to change the order of the calls, but the time zones dictated that Australia always went before Japan.

Whatever I experience in life or the workplace, I choose to flow with it—that makes it so much easier and interesting, and it allows me to achieve my goals faster. Don't label everything as "difficult," but easy or realistic. People are not just a physical body. They are feelings and energy. See it and sense it. You can sense and know their tendencies, and what they will do next. Watch their feelings and comprehend them. See how the feelings and energy flow, and you can see how events will unfold into the future.

ACCEPT everything that happens and move on. Don't linger, and don't plot useless revenge. If you think you have lost, quickly move on, and leave the experience behind you. Once there was a company I wanted to join, a move that would have been a game-changer in my career. I interviewed for two roles; one got filled by an internal candidate and the other the hiring manager thought I wasn't a fit for. Three months later, another role opened that was much more senior and suited to my needs. The universe was saying, "Just wait, the right role is coming your way," and it did.

Sometimes it seems like things are not going our way. Just be patient and have confidence: the seed you have planted will eventually come to fruition.

ASSOCIATES

There is a saying that goes, "Tell me who your best friends are, and I will tell you who you are."

Following the wind, you must evaluate your company and your influences, as a form of strategizing. When you associate with people of poor repute, you tarnish your branding. Don't associate with people who cut corners and cheat. Don't associate with people who are negative or bring you down. Be wary of tolerating mediocrity, lest you become mediocre yourself. If you want to lose weight, make friends with people who like to go to the gym. If you want to become a millionaire, hang around people with a lot of money. Life is too short to associate with people who will take us backward from our unyielding path toward success. Find people who are successful in your areas of interest and start to hang out in their circles. Keep the company of the people you want to aspire to be.

I'm sure you've heard of the samurai. Well, this celebrated class of warriors had a code of ethics and rules. The seven samurai virtues are:

- Righteousness
- Courage
- Benevolence
- Respect
- Honesty
- Honor
- Loyalty

Keep these principles in mind when seeking company, and mold yourself according to these principles as well.

I've seen many people lose very good jobs by cheating on their expenses. It is trivial to get fired over expenses, and yet it happens. You want to avoid getting caught up in bad habits. Often, if there is a culture of corruption in an organization, is it easy to get pressured into committing these acts yourself. Distance yourself from such cultures and such people as much as you can. Additionally, take special care when it comes to forming relationships with people in your workplace. If you are married, you don't enter a romantic or sexual relationship with someone other than your spouse. If you are single, but the other person is married, the same rule applies—especially if the other person is a co-worker. Keeping relationships in the workspace cordial and professional is vital, especially if you are in a leadership position and people follow your example.

If you expect your team to work hard and produce excellence, you must do so yourself. It is best to develop good social relationships with your workers, and let them know that you are their equal. There is no better inspiration than seeing the boss down in the trenches working alongside everyone else. By doing this, you will earn the respect of your team and instill that same hardworking energy among the team.

MEETINGS

Most companies have no strategy or rules when it comes to meetings, which results in a high number of completely unproductive meetings. The worst sin I see within meetings is the complete lack of action taken after they end. If nothing happens after the meeting, the meeting itself was probably a waste of time. Do not underestimate the damage done by a poor meeting. A meeting with eight members of your staff that is not efficient wastes what is, in essence, a whole "person day" of efficiency.

Have an agenda decided for every meeting and share it with all attendees ahead of time. Assign someone to take notes and list action items. If there is no agenda at the start, go to the whiteboard and write down the agenda and meeting goals in bullet points and get buy-in from the attendees. Not all meetings need minutes taken, but all meetings should have a list of actions that are sent out to each participant after the meeting. Rarely should meetings end without some sort of action, and all customer meetings should end with actionable items.

Meetings don't need to be confined to an air-conditioned room around a table. For several hundreds of years, the shoguns in Japan would hold meetings with their subordinates while strolling around their gardens. Sometimes I do meetings where I will go for a one-hour walk outside with one or two people instead of just sitting in the same old meeting. These meetings are usually far more effective and get the members some much-needed fresh air and exercise.

Once, I had an employee who was struggling with personal and work issues, and he wanted to meet. I told him to meet me at 7:30 a.m., and we went for a walk for 45 minutes. In that 45 minutes, we made enormous progress in getting to the core of the issues bothering him, and he repeatedly told me it was the best meeting he ever had. If you have a conference call, put your headset on and go for a walk instead of sitting at your desk. Often a change of scenery, fresh air, and exercise can bring a fresh perspective to your thought process.

For the brave, meetings can be kicked off by having everyone take three deep breaths at the start. I often use this for larger and more important meetings. This does many positive things. It gets people to stop looking at their devices. It increases the amount of oxygen in the lungs to help wake everyone up. Having everyone breathing at the same time puts them in sync. It also helps focus everyone's attention on the actual meeting. However, you'll want to have a few people in the meeting that you know will buy into it to help get everyone to follow along.

CHAPTER 6

AIR BOOK

"IN THE MIDST OF MOVEMENT AND CHAOS KEEP STILLNESS INSIDE OF YOU."

DEEPAK CHOPRA

AIR BOOK

Think of Air as nothingness and emptiness. Emptiness does not mean something is lacking; rather, it implies pure potentiality. There are always infinite possibilities around us. The emptier and clearer we become, the more we can see, connect, and take advantage of every possibility and opportunity.

The more baggage and negativity we can remove from our lives, the more emptiness is left behind which can be filled with something better. In your day-to-day life, if you associate with underachievers, you may sink to their level. If you remove those people from your life, however, you will have the time and openness to meet people who can be a more positive influence on your life. Ultimately the Zen masters achieve enlightenment by completely emptying their minds and removing all impurities, which results in stillness, contentment, and peace. Arriving at true emptiness allows you to keep a steady and balanced mind and spirit as you go out into battle in the business world. You are no longer distracted by random thoughts as they race through your mind. It may be easy to have a calm mind while sitting alone in morning silence, but it is more challenging to keep a calm mind and spirit in the high-stress world of sales and management.

Musashi concluded his *The Book of Five Rings* with the Air book, which included his own personal philosophies and approach to life. Similarly, this section includes my philosophy of mindful leadership which I have developed in all my years working as a sales executive.

MIND BODY SPIRIT

If your body is broken down, then you will never have the stamina and energy to reach your full potential. Many successful businesspeople have their physical being in balance. If you master your body, you will have an easier path towards getting the rest of your personal and work life under control.

This may sound like stereotypical advice, but eating healthily can take you a long way. What you put in your body reflects who you are. Avoid processed food and eat lots of fresh foods, including fruits and vegetables. If you like meat, eat meat. Don't smoke and don't drink too much alcohol. Find a routine that fits you. Even just walking is good exercise. Yoga and stretching are important. Stay flexible. Tree branches are stiff and brittle in fall, but supple and pliant in spring. Be like the young bud in the spring and don't forget to breathe. Breathe deeply into your chest and belly. Use 100 percent of your lungs, and don't do shallow breathing.

Don't fear aging, as it is better than the opposite—dying young. As you age, be grateful you get the chance to do so. The more you fight aging and don't accept it, the quicker you will age. Accept it. Getting older is a natural part of the universe. Be grateful you are alive in these times when knowledge of health and medical technology can extend our lives far longer than in previous generations. The future only holds more progress, so the more you age the more you can witness history unfold.

Don't run your body down: that will only make you susceptible to illness. There is a fundamental difference between Eastern and Western medicine. In the West, we think there are germs around us waiting to attack. In the East, it is believed that you must be in optimum health at all times so that even if there are germs around, you will be resilient and will not get sick. When we get tired and run down, that's when the illness is most likely to make its attack.

Western medicine relies heavily on prescriptions for what ails you. If you have a skin rash, your doctor will probably prescribe a pill or strong crème to apply directly to the skin. They ignore the fact that the patient has some sort of imbalance in their life that is causing their rash. Taking a pill will have other side effects and will probably knock them further off balance. It may or may not cure the rash. It may cause another symptom to break forth, which your doctor also has a pill for. Now you are paying a big pharmacy company for two drugs instead of one.

In Eastern medicine, the doctor may notice the patient is eating too much acid and that the body is out of balance. Adding a few vegetables or a protein each week could put the patient back on track and cure the rash. The father of Western medicine himself, Hippocrates, stated: "Let your food be your medicine, and your medicine is your food."

Let me give you another example. When you get a headache, you most likely take some aspirin (or other over-the-counter headache medicine). However, taking a walk, breathing fresh air, and drinking some water will also help get your energy flowing. Walking will get your heart pumping, which will increase the blood flow throughout your whole body. Drinking water will get your digestive system moving and in balance. Fresh air will oxygenize the cells in your body. Think of a stagnant creek—the water becomes polluted and poisoned. But when the water is flowing, it remains fresh. The same principle applies to your blood and your chi (body energy). When you walk or exercise, you are helping your body cleanse itself. Think of your body like an old door in an abandoned house. The hinges on a door that has not been used become rusty and squeak—the same is true for our joints. Stretching and yoga will do wonders to solve this problem. Swimming is also great because it puts less stress on your back and joints, and you get to cheat gravity.

Much of Western medicine is wonderful and there are many great doctors. Just be careful with the medicines that are prescribed. Always ask questions and take time to go on the internet and research what you are putting into your body.

Beyond just taking care of what goes into your body, it is also important to take care of your external appearance. Always attempt to look not only good but also fresh. It is beneficial to study what clothes look best on you in both work and casual situations. Ask others for advice on what looks good for you. Dress for the situation and dress for success. Your clothes convey a lot to the people around you. Dressing in a sloppy way can easily be interpreted as a careless attitude by your higher-ups, which can damage your reputation. Looking good and dressing well can do wonders in subconsciously convincing your customers that every word you say is true.

Body language complements dressing and appearance. Always adopt an "air of confidence." Stand up straight and have good posture—shoulders back, chest out. Think of meeting someone with slumped-over shoulders, looking down at their shoes. They may not be the type of person you would want to work with or sign a contract with. Amy Cuddy, a leader in this field, wrote: "Let your body tell you you're powerful and deserving, and you become more present, enthusiastic and authentically yourself." Dressing well and standing straight tells the world that you are confident and a winner. In a published paper from 2010, Cuddy reported that such posing can change your hormone levels. She reported that the "results of this study confirmed our prediction that posing in high-power nonverbal displays (as opposed to low-power nonverbal displays) would cause neuroendocrine and behavioral changes for both male and female participants: High-power posers experienced elevations in testosterone, decreases in cortisol, and increased feelings of power and tolerance for risk; low-power posers exhibited the opposite pattern."

Lastly, if you don't do it already, learn to smile—a lot. As the saying goes, "Smile and the world smiles too." So, there's nothing like a smile to create a good first impression. A warm and confident smile will put both you and the other person at ease. Make smiling and happiness your default mode and others in your life and who encounter you will also be happy. Smiling is contagious, and the customers would rather sign a contract with a person who smiles.

You only have one chance to make a good first impression. What do people think and feel when they first encounter you? To succeed, you need to have a certain level of gravitas. If you are not confident, just pretending to be confident is a great start.

"PEOPLE WILL FORGET WHAT YOU SAID. PEOPLE WILL FORGET WHAT YOU DID. BUT PEOPLE WILL NEVER FORGET HOW YOU MADE THEM FEEL."

MAYA ANGELOU

EXECUTIVE PRESENCE

Executive presence is a combination of personal traits and external behaviors that create an image of leadership competence and trustworthiness. It's the vibe you give off to the world about your abilities and trustworthiness. It's not about performance or closing a deal. It's whether you signal to the world that you are leadership material, that you're ready to take on responsibility and be rewarded for it. When it comes to presence, people will size you up in three ways:

1. How you act
2. How you communicate
3. How you look

These three things make a world of difference when it comes to showing others that you are capable of. Look for leaders who display executive presence and copy what they do. What qualities and characteristics do they exhibit? How do they conduct meetings? How do they interact with those both above and below them? How do they react to news of a lost deal? Think of yourself as these people even though you are not—yet. People who have a strong presence handle their business professionally and respectably. They have a can-do attitude and don't go around complaining or whining. Focus on the qualities a strong business leader should possess, such as determination and confidence, and act accordingly.

VIBRATIONS & AURA

Albert Einstein said: "Everything in life is vibration." Sound, colors, and even emotions are just wavelengths vibrating at different speeds at the molecular level. Vibes and auras are energy fields surrounding our bodies that we give off to those around us. Often your gut instinct knows immediately if you like someone or not—a large part of that instinct appears because of the aura the other person exudes.

Human vibrations are composed of everything from physical matter to the way you communicate your thoughts. In simple terms, some molecules vibrate faster and some vibrate slower; there are higher vibrations and lower vibrations. When you are vibrating at a higher level, you feel lighter, happier, and more at ease, whereas lower vibrations feel heavy, dark, and confused.

This energy is constantly changing depending on our health, state of mind, and interaction with others. It is best to pay attention to your first impressions of others and steer clear of the people who give off bad vibes. The best sales reps and executives give off an aura of positivity, competency, and trustworthiness.

Identify people you like or who are considered likable. What does their vibe feel like? What characteristics do they have? What actions or activities can you copy? How do they speak, walk, and talk? Now, I am not saying you should just copy someone exactly, but rather, look at the traits that make them a likable person and learn from them. Pay attention to how positive relationships feel as well as the energy that comes from them, then try to emulate them. Additionally, to help you maintain your positive vibes, be aware of your home environment. Your home life has a huge effect on your attitude and aura, as well as your work life.

Becoming aware of your vibrations—and the levels of what surrounds you—allows you to seek opportunities to raise your vibration level. Reading vibes is mostly intuitive. For example, when a person walks into a room, you get an immediate vibe about that person. Is this person giving off good vibes that draw you closer? Or is the person giving off negative vibes and making you want to keep your distance? It happens all around you. When you are, let's say, at the mall and you see someone yelling at a cashier or store employee who is just trying to help, you get a heavy feeling. During the same trip, you witness a mother coddling her newborn baby, and you suddenly have hope for all mankind.

As they can extend outward, when you catch yourself with negative thoughts, just stop and reboot your head. Do not beat yourself up or chastise yourself. Everyone has negative thoughts, but the key is to not dwell on them. Picture something positive, such as your child laughing or something funny that recently happened. We send our vibrations out to the world, and the world then sends vibrations back to us. To move to the next level, we need to raise our perception of what is going on around us. Perception is not just our sense of sight. Seeing is done only with the eyes, but perception involves using your eyes, ears, nose, gut feeling, intuition, internal radar, spirit, and more. It involves reading the room and people.

Be conscious of your thoughts. What you think and feel becomes your reality and your aura. Think beautiful thoughts. Picture yourself working in your dream job on the path to financial independence.

"As you think, you vibrate. As you vibrate, you attract."
Abraham-Hicks

So, how are you vibrating right now?

HUMILITY

Rarely, if ever, should you purposely promote yourself or your work. If you must engage in self-promotion, make sure it is in the form of facts and not bragging. As soon as you start bragging, you become a target for others who want to bring you down. The less you toot your own horn, the quicker you will make progress and get ahead. If you close a deal and proceed to go mentioning it to everyone, people will tire of listening to you and will not want to support your activities. If you achieve success, never brag, and try to give the credit to others that helped you along the way. In this way, the people around you will also make sure you get credit, they will do your promotion for you.

Each culture is different. In the West, especially the United States, people talk about themselves all the time. In Japan and other countries in Asia, they generally don't promote themselves and are self-deprecating. Too much bragging almost always backfires, and you lose respect instead of gaining it. Keep the culture of your organization, and the wider culture of the country you are living in, at the back of your mind when gauging how to act.

Sometimes it is good to keep a little cockiness about you just to keep your edge and let others know you are a player. We can all learn from the great Benjamin Franklin who wrote his 13 habits and included humility as the very last one. He said he didn't make much progress, but he had learned to feign humility.

When you pretend to know it all and never admit to your mistakes, you model behavior that can have negative consequences for yourself and your entire organization. Conversely, when you are self-aware enough to openly admit missteps and concede that you still have plenty of room to learn, you turn mistakes into learning opportunities and permit people to be collaborative without fear of appearing unqualified.

To begin to increase your self-awareness, seek feedback on your performance from others by asking good questions and listening without justifying or defending your actions. Remember, organizations benefit far more from leaders who take responsibility for what they don't know than from leaders who pretend to know it all. When the staff comes to you with advice, listen to them. Keep an open-door policy.

LEADING & COACHING

Without a strong and competent manager, even your most competent reps will start to disengage. Great leaders not only bring in great reps but they also counsel, coach, motivate, and create a climate of teamwork amongst these reps.

The most important thing you can do as a manager is to listen to your reps. Find out what motivates everyone. It is not all just about money, which is the old cliché – sales reps only care about commission checks. Salespeople want to connect with their boss and teammates. Even if, for some reps, commissions are the number one motivating factor, find out what else makes them tick. Do they like to be praised in front of their peers for success? Do they want flexibility in working hours because they have children in daycare? Do they want a promotion? Maybe a different vertical market to sell to? More autonomy? Training? One thing everyone wants is to be listened to. They want to feel that they matter. Listen to your reps and find out what motivates them. Find out what their interests are. If you have your reps make a business plan, you can ask them what their goals and aspirations are. You will find that money is rarely mentioned as a factor.

It is amazing how priceless the old "pat on the back" is to raise the motivation level of reps and the team. Get into the habit of praising them in private as well as public, as it will help you connect with them each as individuals and as a team, and you will be rewarded handsomely with loyalty.

POWER OF BAKED BREAD AND BIRTHDAYS

I had an amazing Japanese sales director who would celebrate the birthday of every person who reported to her. She would get each member of the team to chip in a couple of dollars (¥200 in that case), and someone would buy a cake and candles. The team would get together and celebrate the birthday and eat together. It created a sense of "team"—in a tribal way, to an extent. It was a simple yet powerful team-building tool.

Another simple yet powerful action I have taken during the past 20 years is to bring freshly baked bread or cookies into the office. I would share them with people on the team, as well as any others whom I communicated with often in the company, such as sales support people, billing people, and legal folks. I would bring the bread to work and share it with my teammates, and it helped me realize how much people like receiving a gift out of the blue. There is almost a religious or ceremonial aspect of receiving bread and taking part in eating it together. Think of it like the communion in a Catholic church.

One time, I had a senior Japanese engineer/product executive who was very stubborn and did not ever want to make any concessions to the sales team to help us do our jobs effectively. This was a problem since I had signed a contract worth several million dollars with a very large and powerful US IT company that wanted us to meet all their demands immediately. The Japanese exec would often show up early in the office and I would always make sure I had some bread for him. This simple act got him to feel more warmly toward me and helped us make more of a connection. I was eventually able to be much more productive with this guy than anyone else in the office.

Recently, I took over a sales director role in Tokyo managing a team of sales professionals and sales engineers, all of whom are Japanese except one. In my first couple of days on the job, I could feel the stress in the team as we sat at our desks. The Japanese team had been seriously underperforming and was already under a lot of stress. Now they had a new American boss they didn't know anything about. They didn't know if I understood Japanese business practices, if I was going to start firing the underperformers without first getting to know them and giving them a chance, and if I was a hard ass. Around day three, I brought in some banana bread my wife had made, and I was the first person in the office. As each member went to their desk and was getting set up for the day, I stopped by, used their first name, and offered them some bread. Each person was very happy to receive the bread, and the office atmosphere later that morning was much more relaxed. These were the first seeds of developing our new team and new team culture.

CONCLUSION

In 2017, while I was the general manager of NetSuite at Oracle Japan, I was delighted to be asked to become one of the five founders of the Mindfulness Project. Oracle Japan had more than 2,000 employees and, as a result, there was a full-time doctor on staff. That company doctor noticed that many employees were suffering from work-related stress, resulting in headaches, stomach pain, and other ailments. He would recommend aspirin and other medication, but more and more employees were asking for a remedy without taking any pills. The doctor contacted the HR department, which in turn decided to create a program based on Google's "Search inside Yourself" course. Because of my role in creating this course, I've led many employees down the route of mindful sales, and now I've written this book so that anyone and everyone can become mindful in their careers at any time or place.

These past few years, there has been a strong shift in the market and society towards mindfulness. Employers now seek workers who are more connected to themselves, which means that candidates with the qualities of self-control, mindful awareness, and emotional restraint earn more money and climb faster.

Terms such as "work–life balance" have become popular for a reason: more mindful people are better leaders and better workers. Without mindfulness, the different aspects of your life float disconnect from one another, leading to a disoriented mental state. Mindfulness helps tie everything together, allowing you to make one small positive change at a time, which eventually results in a holistic improvement for your life as a whole.

Mindful sales leaders are always aware of the moment and are mentally present while interacting with customers. When the customer starts talking, they remain quiet and listen carefully. They manage to close deals because they ask good questions, show empathy, take active notes, follow up on promised actions, and build a good rapport. Practicing mindful meditation may not guarantee automatic sales, but it does increase your prospects because you learn to be more customer-focused and engaged with the present moment.

Recall the most rewarding moment you've had in your business career. You're probably thinking of the time you took part in a great team, which cooperated and worked together in harmony to achieve something special. When all is said and done, the most successful sales leaders are the ones who are in touch with the mindful and spiritual aspects of their job. This is an often-overlooked aspect of this, or any other, job. Yet, it is a critical aspect that will pay huge dividends in the quality of your job and your life. Keep learning and growing every day and miracles will appear!

For more information visit:
https://mind-over-sales.com/

Made in the USA
Coppell, TX
17 October 2021